To Joe & June

I hope you both
enjoy the
of all happened.

Best Wishes

Joe Ross

I BELIEVE THERE IS NO DEATH

Joseph D. Ross Jr., M.D.

I Believe There Is No Death

Library of Congress
Cataloging-in-Publication Data
ISBN 1-56167-844-9

Library of Congress Card Catalog Number:
2004090648

Used with permission of The Helen Steiner Rice™ Foundation, Cincinnati, Ohio
"Before You Can Dry Another's Tears, You Too Must Weep!"
©1965 The Helen Steiner Rice™ Foundation—All Rights Reserved
"This I Believe"
©1972 The Helen Steiner Rice™ Foundation—All Rights Reserved

Published by

8019 Belair Road, Suite 10
Baltimore, Maryland 21236

Manufactured in the United States of America

Death be not proud, though some have called thee
Mighty and dreadful. for thou art not soe,
For, those, whom thou think'st, thou dost overthrow,
Die not, poore death, nor yet canst thou kill me...

—John Donne
Anglican priest and poet

*To
my wife, Eileen.
Thank you for making
my life beautiful
and to
our six children,
the pearls of our world.*

The Mystery In Translating Love

Is That It Has No Words

~

It Is Song Without Refrain

Doctrine Without Text

It Is Poetry Without Verse

Prophecy Without Voice

~

For It Is Simply Our Legacy

Bequeathed By Love Itself

To Joe,
A Man who
has Known
Love truly.
Bless You!
Nancy

Nancy Weyrauch 99

Contents

PROLOGUE

As chief medical examiner of Dutchess County in New York State for 18 years, I face death almost every day; it is a part of life. The inevitability of death is assessed in poems, essays, mysteries, and, of course, in our daily newspapers. Death holds a certain fascination for us, as long as it's not our own.

I write, not about life and death, but about death and life, because I have come to the conclusion that there is no death. Death as we interpret it, is not the end, oblivion. It is the beginning, the beginning of a new, more beautiful and exciting life, a life which has no end. Ask many loved ones of people who have suffered tragic and untimely deaths, and they will attest to exactly this same revelation. I have encountered their – and my own – fascinating after-death communications (ADCs) and near-death experiences (NDEs), and here I write of such experience. I write with the perspective of a physician, an obstetrician who for 25 years dealt with birth and the miracle of life, and as a medical examiner who has seen the end of physical life, leading me always to the same conclusion: there is no death!

I investigated hundreds of deaths and mystical experiences, and I experienced myself the total personal helplessness and extreme depth of sorrow that overwhelms us when faced with indescribable loss. Six years ago such a deep and personal loss invaded my very soul when my true and only love, my wife Eileen, died of an extremely unusual and unlikely cause. She, along with our six adult children, had given me the most beautiful and satisfying life. It was totally shattered when she became ill on March 20, 1995. She went into a coma and died exactly one year to the day later. Eileen's death created an overwhelming emptiness and loneliness in my life, which continues even to this day.

My world changed; the best part of me died. In the

struggle to live without her, I am learning to understand that this is but a hiatus – we will be together again and forever.

There is a universal "switchboard" that transmits messages to our world from our eternal world instantly, accurately, and with a great abundance of love. There are thousands of spiritual communications (ADCs) enhancing our lives. The facts are indisputable.

However, people generally don't broadcast these wonderful signs. They quietly carry them in their hearts, realizing life is forever. Take my brother-in-law Jim, who as everyone agrees, is definitely a no-nonsense guy. It is over 30 years ago since this mystical event happened to him, and I just heard about it. Jim was sitting at his mother's bedside as she was in the last stages of cancer of the pancreas. She took one last deep breath and then stopped breathing. Jim reached for her hand, and at that very moment, a glow left her body, rose to the ceiling and out of the room. It was a definite glow, perfectly visible and clear to Jim. He said nothing about this event to anyone, but has carried it in his heart all these years.

Jim is not the only person to see or hear something as a loved one "crossed over." My sister Nancy heard a definite "whoosh" at 4:00 a.m. when our mother died as we were keeping our vigil with her. My sister Mary and I heard nothing. However, if you read about ADC experiences, you will find that other loved ones have left this world with that very same "whoosh."

Anyone who has read about Dr. Elizabeth Kubler-Ross's fascinating accounts of ADCs and NDEs (near-death experiences), must be familiar with her amazing experience of meeting with a dead client. She had the client write a note to their good friend. Dr. Ross said, "The scientist in me had to have concrete proof of her appearance or they really would think I had lost it."

Then from my own research comes an experience that

happens so often that doubt of its authenticity is not even an honest consideration. Mrs. Charter, whom I interviewed for my book, awoke early one morning at 3:30 a.m: "I felt like an elephant was sitting on my chest. I could hardly catch my breath. Then it passed. I started to think about my brother who lived in Texas and then fell back asleep. About 6:00 a.m. I got the call. My brother had died. I said, "When?" and they said, "Twenty after three."

ADCs come in every conceivable form. We may be physically touched by our own deceased loved ones. Or we see, hear, and even smell them: my sister Nancy one day, six months after my father had died and she had cleaned and aired out his room, suddenly smelled the tobacco smoke there on the second floor as if he was sitting smoking his cigarettes. We are warned of coming events, have validation and evidence of circumstances, and receive solid token gifts that are left for us from the other side:

1) From Dad in a dream comes, "Congratulations, daughter. I see you are expecting and everything will be fine." Poor girl has no idea as yet that she is with child.

2) Another message (dream) from another Dad: Your husband has been stealing money from the business. He has a separate secret bank account at precisely which bank and exactly to the penny the amount of money in the account.

3) A special toy appears in the baby's room – one which Dad had wanted to buy before he suddenly and unexpectedly died.

4) Captain's bars appear from a devoted soldier brother, when he showed up late one night from the afterlife and told his sister, "I am well and we will be together again." He then vanished. The captain's bars were found firmly pressed into her hand.

5) From the six Russian cosmonauts during their fifth month on the Sayuz 7 Space Station comes this event: Suddenly they saw a brilliant orange glow. When their eyes became adjusted to the glow they clearly saw seven giant figures – angels – flying alongside the space station. This lasted about 10 minutes before they whisked away. Were the cosmonauts imagining or hallucinating? Exactly 12 days later the brilliant orange glow and the seven exciting figures (wings and all) returned and then there was no doubt. They all agreed.

6) Prof. S. Ralph Harlow of Smith College and his wife were walking hand-in-hand through the woods near Ballardvale, Massachusetts, when, "we heard the murmur of muted voices in the distance. The voices came closer and closer. Then this amazing phenomenon occurred right before our eyes. Floating by us was a group of glorious creatures that glowed with spiritual beauty. There were six of them, young, beautiful women in white garments engaged in earnest conversation. They floated on past us with a graceful motion giving no indication of our presence. When I asked my wife to tell me what she saw, she described to me exactly in every respect what I had seen and heard. This phenomenon has truly altered our very thinking."

Of course, there are many accounts of religious apparitions which have occurred all over the world from England to France to Italy to Egypt, Japan, to Africa, and even to the USA. Some are very famous, as Fatima and Lourdes, which were depicted in motion pictures. One of the most widely publicized and witnessed apparitions occurred in Zeitoun, Egypt, a suburb of Cairo. An apparition of the Virgin Mary first appeared on April 2, 1968 and continued to reappear during the next two years. It was witnessed by millions of people and photographed thousands of times, even by many professional photographers, and also investigated by the secular media all over the world, including *The New York Times*.

I could go on and on about the thousands of other world mysteries and experiences by ordinary people, but for now, let me introduce my own personal transformation to complete faith in God's eternal plan for all of us. Therefore this book is, I believe, a collaboration between my wife Eileen and me. Through God, and out of my wife's love from above, and out of my human need, I have come to understand that there is truly this precious continuation of our love forever. I, and the other people I have met who have shared their stories with me, have been exquisitely touched from the other dimension of eternal life. I present to you this evidence for life after death with my deepest faith and integrity. Treat it with the same.

Joseph D. Ross Jr., M.D.

ACKNOWLEDGEMENTS

This book is my heart, but it would not have made one beat without the myriad great old friends and wonderful newfound friends who helped and encouraged me along the way. They are too numerous to count. I must, however, mention several special people who contributed to my faith and my book. I pray I do not leave anyone out.

My beautiful Eileen filled my life with signs of love and inspiration even after she left this world. My six children, each and every one of them, were always there to erase any doubt that would crop up in a lonely, saddened man. Their introduction exhibits our closeness and family love. My daughter Nancy Ross was the computer expert. Without her, I doubt that the roots of this writing would have blossomed into its final growth. Patrick Herrmann, my grandson, was instrumental in helping with every design and lady bug that popped up here and there. Nancy Weyrauch's beautiful poem is a fitting beginning to my story.

My deepest gratitude to those of faith and understanding who contributed to this book. I want to mention especially Adelaide Vaughn, Sheila Fuimarello, my sister Nancy Ross, Betty Bogholtz, Brian Petro, Ann McVeigh, Kim O'Brien, Penny Breda, Joanne Mizerak, Joan DiGiacomo, Mary Francisco, Evelyn Charter, Sandra Alley, Nancy Miller Haas, Della O'Leary, and Al Beres.

Also, special thanks to Alan C. Reese, Managing Editor, and Camille, Sallie, Julie, Barbara, and Donna of Noble House for your faith and confidence in my very personal endeavor.

INTRODUCTION

Nancy

For my Dad, it had to come out, and here it is. So much indescribable pain, so much incredible wonder, all stemming from the same singular woman and the events of her life, death, and continuing presence. I don't know if it was prescience or simple child's attachment, but since I was very little, when I'd say my prayers at night, I would always pray, "Please, Lord, let my parents enjoy their old age together." But the decades of making this plea were to no avail, because my mother died young, and she died an exhausting, humiliating, heart-wrenching death. I can still see her laughing with us in the kitchen in the good years, about how Dad would be a funny old man as they ambled together in the Poconos, a laugh full of tenderness and love. And I can still see her sitting nearly catatonic in the den, the occasional look of horrified bewilderment clouding her face the only sign that she was still in there. And now I see my Dad, whispering to her spirit as he moves from room to room, keeping his connection to her his mainstay throughout these years of loneliness. This is my father's story of how his faith in God and love that does not end found actual flapping wings, crackling sound, and human solidarity in his daily struggle to live in this world when my Mom left for the next one.

The literature is full of tales of mighty wind and fantastic ghosts, booming voices and slamming doors. Impressive. Thought-provoking. Dad's tale is not of spine tingles. It's better, because it's a tale of every single family. We all have a great grandmother who knew things were going to happen before they did, or a cousin who saw a beloved standing in the doorway at the same time this person died a thousand miles away. We have friends whose deceased fathers tapped them on the shoulder as they were falling asleep at the wheel, and clocks that stopped inexplicably at significant times, and a sudden warm feeling of uncanny comfort as we sat weeping in the garden.

At my mother's funeral, two brothers who had lost their own young mother years before, each went up separately to my brother Joe. John said, "Joe, it gets better with time." Minutes later, Eddie stood beside him and said, "Joe, it never gets better." They are so right. It is entirely both. But my father's personal stories, and his passionate, honest writing of them, are a gift for each of us straddling these human and spiritual experiences.

Joe

In the (unbiased, of course) opinion of her children, my Mom had it right. The house that she kept was clean but it wasn't always neat. You could put your feet on the furniture, set up your papers and crayons on the dining room table, and yes, you could even lie down or watch TV in the living room. You could play Superman and jump off of the couch if she wasn't looking, and, I suspect, even at times when she was. She would rather sit at the kitchen table and listen to us talk about our day, or go to the diner and laugh about nothing, than spend time on pretense.

Not that she missed the important details... My brown bag lunch in grade school had sliced tomatoes separated from the sandwich in a plastic sandwich bag, because otherwise the bread would get soggy. A few people laughed as I constructed my lunch. I asked how THEIR bread tasted and the conversation was over.

As a teen I would come home on frigid winter nights in my old car with no heater. I'd go to my room and the electric blanket covering my bed was turned on. My bones and heart warmed instantly. She never missed a night.

Yes, in the opinion of her children, my Mom had it right. She lives on through all of us and our children, but that is our spirit and not what this book is about. This book is about experiences and evidence that my and others' loved ones continue, not just in our hearts, but truly do CONTINUE.

Do I think there is more after this life? Yes, I absolutely do. Do I know the details? No. Do I think that certain interpretations of communications are a stretch? Yes, I do, but I also see others as too clear and specific to be anything other. Do I think I'll sort it all out before it is my time? Not likely, but for now, that's OK. For now, we can take it in with our hearts and our minds. All of us, at some point, will know with certainty one day – I believe it will be good.

Eileen

In March of 1996 my life and the lives of my family were turned upside-down by the sickness and death of my mother. Growing up Roman Catholic, my twelve years of Catholic school and church had engrained a sense of spirit and "God" in me. I believed in the idea of heaven and life everlasting. However, all of that information was very much on the surface for me until I was pounded with this direct experience of death. After Mom died I had to believe that there REALLY was life after death. That Mom's spirit still existed somewhere and that she could still hear me, relate to me, be a guide somehow like she used to be was vital information at the time. It's not as if I believed that she had died and there was no part of her left anywhere. I always believed she could hear me and was still "on my side." But after Dad started reading all the books on after-death communications and psychic mediums, I began learning more about all the amazing research that has been done in these areas. The stories Dad would tell us about what he had just read would sometimes simply blow my mind. I never realized how much information was out there, or how many more people were so interested in death, after-death issues, near-death experiences, and the like. I began to "wake-up" to the signs. Instead of only believing that Mom could hear me, but I couldn't "hear" her, I started allowing myself to open up to her communications WITH me and others, including family and friends. Some of the signs that I consider as Mom saying hello may seem absolutely ridiculous to others, however they are becoming more concrete to me everyday. Why do we automatically assume everything is a coincidence? And what is the harm in believing a loved one is communicating with us anyway? My belief in the idea of heaven and life everlasting isn't the same as it was when I was younger; it is bigger and better for my life now! I owe this sense of faith very much to my father who has demonstrated the same need to know more. The stories and the books he has shared with all of us have been very healing for me. I think we never really know where our beliefs and faith lie until we are directly confronted with a challenge such as the death of a loved one. I have a much wider view of life in general than I had a few years ago after sharing in Dad's research. It has brought more peace to my life. I still miss Mom immensely – the whole family does. But the sense of peace and connectedness that comes along with knowing that our spirit lives on even after our bodies die is a critical aspect to healing and in living life to its fullest. I hope this book will help others to heal and find peace as well.

Theresa

With my thoughts and feelings about my Mom and about life in Heaven, I go back and forth between unbearable sadness and infinite thankfulness, with coexisting feelings of anger and fear and love and peace. It is very hard to juggle all of these emotions at once, but that is what I do. I am forever grateful for being blessed with such amazing parents and wonderful siblings. They say there is strength in numbers, and this is very true. But I still feel alone – an alone that comes when your Mother dies, when the love of your Mother is gone from your life in this world. It is that love that reaches down from Heaven that keeps me going, but keeps me missing her so. It is the joy she gave to my life that makes me smile and brings me to tears. It is knowing she is always with me that gives each day that special magic, and yet her absence that keeps the dark clouds over my heart. She gave me so much, but the fact that she was taken away leaves an ache so deep. I would never try to assume to understand God's plans or ways. He gave me more than I deserve in so many ways through so many people. But with that gift comes the inevitable cost of trying to get through this world when time is up for this part of life and you are left with a void that cannot be filled. Your faith is truly tested, but I also know the faith I have is what gives balance to sorrow with comfort. I know that some people say that "faith" is just a crutch, but I firmly respond that my faith is not a crutch. My faith is a gift. I know my Mom is now with God in Heaven. I know this. In knowing that my Mom is with God, I know that anything is possible. I know it more now, since she died, because she has been with me in ways I never thought possible. She has saved my life. She has helped keep my heart from breaking beyond repair. I have been given the gift of her ability to reach down from Heaven so I am reminded that she is there. I will try to hold fast to the love I receive from people here in my life and from people that send their love from the after life. It isn't easy to have to miss the people we love. This book my Dad has written is just one of the many reasons I am so proud of him, and I know that my Mom is proud of him, too. It is not supposed to make it easier to live in this world without your loved ones, but perhaps it can empower you with the knowledge that your loved ones still live. That won't take away the tears, but it will help you to see through them, or in this case, type through them. I love you Mom.

<u>Jim</u>

 1995 started out with such promise. My wife, Jean, and I had decided to move back up to New York from outside Philadelphia after 6 years of constantly traveling the New Jersey Turnpike for holidays, birthdays, parties, first haircuts, or whatever the event may have been. We recruited my brother to help us move (as is the custom in our family whenever someone moves – which is a story in itself). We packed up our stuff, our 1½ -year-old son, and were very excited to finally be closer to our families. I had a new job, another baby on the way, and things were looking good. Jean and I enjoyed the "stopping in" on my folks (her parents had the privilege housing us in our transition), and the impromptu trips to the diner. There was something about my mom that always made you feel at ease. She truly enjoyed and loved her family. All that changed on March 20, 1995 when my mom became, what turned out to be, terminally ill.

The remainder of the year was a roller coaster of emotions for everyone in our family. Although there were some minor improvements in my mother's condition, all were minimal and short-lived. However, we experienced the closeness that tragedy brings, as we all would stop our lives and rush to the house/hospital whenever there was the slightest change in her status. I remember cringing every time the phone would ring – anticipating "the call." Finally, a year to the day after taking ill, my mom died. It was the one night out of the entire year I decided to stay the night at my parents' house. I held her hand and watched her die.

Being raised a good Catholic boy, I knew my mom was going directly to "heaven." She brought up six children, packed ten thousand lunches, and was about as good a person as you would ever find. Personally, I don't need any proof that there is life after death, a better place: heaven. I believe this to be true and it is the foundation of my faith. I know my father believes this to be true as well. However, the loss of his wife and companion for almost 40 years was more than he could bear. He needed something more tangible to help him through sorrow and loss. His journey into "life after death" has been a catharsis and has uncovered countless instances of communications and experiences that can't be swept under the rug. For those of you looking for that "something more," I'm sure you will find some solace. For those of you who may not believe, here's some food for thought.

Nick

 Who lives on this earth without experiencing the death of a loved one? Unless you die young and have lived with little connection and love, it is an event you can't escape. Life is filled with ongoing patterns of connection and loss. Yet death often brings about the deepest, most difficult losses we face.

In my work at a grief support agency, I have been with

hundreds of children and adults who are living with the recent death of a parent, spouse, or other loved one. We are careful to explain the concreteness of death to children, stating that when a person we love *dies* it means that person's *body* stops working – just like a bird or spider, when their bodies are dead they don't eat or play or move ever again. When someone we love dies we often feel many feelings and it can hurt beyond measure. Kids understand this, and, in fact, have much to teach us about grief. They also have much to teach us about connections that continue after someone has died. For them it doesn't have to be anomalous or mysterious; it just is. The stories I hear from the children, like those in this book, confirm again and again that death is not the end.

A month after my 28th birthday my mother died. My Mom's death left a hole in my life that will never be filled. Her love and support along with my Dad's was extraordinary – the greatest gift I have ever received. The death of my mother, the loss of her presence and all the concrete love and support that came with it, is the greatest loss I have ever experienced even though I feel her spirit with me still. For my father the death of my Mom was unfathomable. It was as if a piece of him was ripped off. He did not know who he was without her.

As this book demonstrates, who he has become without her is a representation of hope. You can't stand for long in line at a bank or a check-out counter and talk with my father without feeling that hope and finding it in yourself. The stories he has gathered in addition to his own are not unlike the countless stories you will hear if you inquire among your own friends and families. I too believe that death is not the absolute end for any of us. The love my mother and father shared in this world was extraordinary. I believe the connection between them that continues to live is real. May the stories in this book awaken your own hope and openness to communications with loved ones who have died.

CHAPTER ONE

HOW BEAUTIFUL IT WAS AND HOW SHORT IT SEEMED!

"The measure of love is to love without measure."
—*St. Francis de Sales*

It has now been six years since my wife, Eileen, my love, my earthly angel, died at the relatively young age of 64 of a rare combination of medical conditions that I could not, in my wildest dreams, have envisioned. She was very sick for a year, and died on March 20, 1996, exactly one year to the day when she contracted an unknown type of acute meningitis which led to numerous complications.

However, this is not actually about those devilish and nightmarish circumstances. It is about one man's transformation from ambivalent, superficial faith and love to a gut-wrenching and deep understanding of unconditional faith and love. I will honestly bare my heart and soul about my deep unending love for my wife, Eileen, and the absolutely amazing and beautiful ways she reached me from her unknown, perfect world. I hope that my journey and experience will give people pause for thought and help them to understand the "tragedy" of death as the first step to God's promise of a paradise and wondrous, everlasting life. One of the visionaries of Medjugorje (where apparitions of the Virgin Mary have been seen) stated, "If men only knew what awaits them in eternity, they would do everything in their power to change their lives."

But, please, wait! This is not about religion and tradition. This is about a wandering soul and even now an empty, lonely, incomprehensible and unending sadness. It is about a living, growing belief in life forever and a truly beautiful gift of love. It is about climbing a steep, sharp, rocky mountain of emptiness and despair alone, and poking through the clouds to an everlasting sunshine and joy. And, yet, with this slow-growing understanding enveloping my heart, I still cry every day at the most unlikely and unwanted times. It is still impossible to fully describe the wretched hollowness, the intensely burning hurt in my life, the utter despair without her, that I wonder how my heart doesn't explode from missing her. Even with this total emptiness in my life, I can see that I have come a long way on this very steep road, and even though my grief is impenetrable and my life has an unfillable void, I can now believe in and see a future for us of overwhelming joy.

Therefore, this lonely, intense journey is about thoughts, ideas, discussions, conversations, philosophical explorations, psychic phenomena, and research. All of which have led me to an inner peace. It has given me absolute realization that, "Hey! There is more out there." There is more than we simple humans are willing and possibly able to assimilate into our hearts and minds. It is about me knowing—absolutely knowing—that I will see my love again, truly in another beautiful and all-loving world. This journey is about believing, to the depth of my being, that once our God has created each and every one of us, he has deemed that we won't die; we can't die; even if we want to completely destroy ourselves; we can't die! We have been created to live with Him forever, for eternity. This I believe. For me, this I know. Believing is seeing; believing is knowing.

I hope the story of my transformation and my understanding of our world and life might give others a willingness to explore their souls, an openness to think of God's creation and His perfect love for us. Perhaps my experience will help others understand and be comforted at the unfathomable loss of a loved one, since no one can aptly describe such an exquisite emptiness, and all of us will suffer this deep-seated anguish.

During my journey over the past six years, I have seen and felt happenings (coincidences) so numerous and obvious that they could not be rejected. I have experienced wonderful signs that cannot be discarded as ridiculous, impossible, unbelievable, or even unscientific. As a physician, trained in science, and a medical examiner who has dealt with death on a daily basis, I am not easily influenced. Throughout this book, I will quote from reputable physicians, psychologists, philosophers, poets, writers, scientists, and just plain "Bills" who also search, feel, and understand, thus giving credence to the exciting other world of the unknown and misunderstood. I do not look to change attitudes, beliefs, tradition, or non-beliefs. I do not suggest that you believe in anything whatsoever. However, I hope you will read on in good conscience and with integrity and wisdom. (Wisdom is the insight which goes beyond the perceptions of our five animal senses.)

Bear with me, any skeptics of all ages—from those who knew the earth was flat to those who persecuted Galileo—for I truly hope that my experiences and journey will help to fill the inner void of others. I hope my evolving thoughts and feelings will help in the Western cultural struggle over the fear of death and dying. Maybe we should reevaluate our lives in a world of hypocrisy, self-indulgence, and greed, a world where love has been divested of its beauty, and look to a rebirth of conscience and compassion.

My story begins with all the good times of my life and a superficial understanding of life and death. As a young man, there was total immersion in the beauty of my marriage, family, work, and play, each one innocently beautiful in my almost perfect world. (I continue to thank my God every day for such a magnificent gift.) Personal and wrenching sorrow did not touch me, only at a distance. It did, however, touch the life of my beautiful wife, with the early death at age 56 of her mother and with the death of other close members of her family, including her father. I wonder and question with all my love for her, did I really understand her tortured heart and was I enough support for her? If I was not a pillar of strength for her, she did not let on. She did, however, without one ounce of doubt, know of my overwhelming love and care for her in every way. She knew in every fiber of her being, as did I, that our love and marriage reached the top of Mt. Everest and touched the sun. For the two of us, with our deep inner feelings, our quiet peace and joy, our complete confidence in each other, and our total gift of each to the other, there was only pure happiness and contentment in our lives. Our love was a divine gift.

I must tell you about my wife, Eileen, so that you can better understand our life together and my unyielding loss. But how do you write about a friend, companion, wife, lover, mother—an earthly angel who truly made your life "heaven on earth"—who made your world one of pure contentment and joy, who made you feel totally wonderful just being in her presence and who has now gone to a "special and inexpressible place of joy, an imperishable inheritance?" (Words of St. Peter) How do mere words describe such an overwhelmingly beautiful woman? I can't help it. I can't stop. Tears well up in my eyes every day from the indescribable emptiness in my heart and soul without her. "My sweetest girl," I called her, who was given God's extraordinary grace in this life and has spread His love unselfishly to so many others. It is said that God is love, and my girl practiced this very love every day of her life.

What is love? Really, what is this intangible thread of life? Love is giving! Love is giving to others without any concern or interest in what you might receive in return. This marvelous woman in my life gave of herself every day, willingly and with joy. She gave of herself to me, to our six children, to her father (who lived with us), to her sister and brothers, and to everyone whom she touched. I thank my God every day for my life with her, for His special gift to me. For it was no coincidence that I met her. (I believe, as did Carl Jung, that there are no coincidences.)

When I returned from the Army Air Corps after World War II, I attended college and my goal was to become a physician. College at that time was made up of a lot of "worldly" veterans as well as a lot of people just out of high school. There was much competition and medical schools were overwhelmed with applications during that period. It took me three years to be accepted into medical school after college. During this time I earned a Master's Degree in science and taught school for a year. I'll never forget that wonderful day in October of 1952 when my mother phoned me at school and told me I had been accepted into medical school. My prayers and dreams had been answered. Little did I know that God had something more wonderful, more fulfilling, more beautiful, in store for me in this same month.

Sometime during that same exciting month I attended a party with friends and met a girl whom I subsequently dated. Later on, my friends and I planned a party with her and her friends at the apartment where they lived. This apartment was the second floor of a house of a very nice and caring family. During this party, as we paired off to dance and get acquainted, I gravitated toward a very pretty, quiet, and sweet young lady, whom I shortly realized was the most wonderful person I had ever met. God touched us with his angel dust and the sparkle never has diminished. I can truly say that when I came to know this naïve, sweet, quiet, and intelligent young woman, I fell uncontrollably and madly in love with her and wanted to spend my life loving and caring for her. It turned out to be too short a time together, but clearly was my heaven and sheer joy in this world. I called her "my sweetest girl" and every day of our lives I told her I loved her, over and over again, and I still do love her with all of the divine love that God gave us. She showed me her love by her caring nature, her beautiful disposition, and the wonderful, thoughtful, and loving way she treated me. I talk to her every day, tell her how much I love her and miss her, and I know that she hears me from that other, special world.

This world changed for me starting on March 20, 1995, and by March 20, 1996, I had lost her to the next life, but I will be with her forever, for eternity. This I believe! You see, we are born to this world, and we die to live forever on the "other side." As my wife said to me, in my cousin's dream, "I am in a better place than I was before." This I do believe, and I can hardly wait to join her, God's most wonderful gift to me.

I have spent six years exploring the possibilities, and I know that we don't die. We were created by Him to be with Him eternally in an ever-loving kingdom of Paradise. God has shown Himself to all of us, but we must be open to perceive His greatness. Men and women of more wisdom than I, from Buddha, to Saints Peter and Paul, to Walt Whitman, to Carl Jung, to Joan of Arc, to our contemporary, Mother Teresa, have felt His greatness, His perfect love, His mercy, and have basked in the beauty of His creation. Whoever your personal God is, He is the same for one and all. He is love and mercy and inexhaustible forgiveness.

Your body, your mortal bones, wear out, get old, stop functioning, but your soul (spirit, consciousness) is then free to grow in the eternal life, a life which "man cannot comprehend nor can he conceive what wonders are in store for him." We have been given (and literally, millions of us have experienced) signs, intuitions, miracles, visions, apparitions, near-death experiences, after-death communications, dream visions, deathbed visions, angels, and on and on—proofs, I believe, that we are eternal beings.

After all, we are products of our culture and environment, which, in our Western society, is decidedly materialistic and essentially very narrow in its perception of reality, and unquestionably that reality is there for only what we see. We have yet to understand that we only see what our culture demands of us, and only know (believe) what society insists we accept. As Dannion Brinkley, who had a near-death experience, so aptly puts it in his extraordinary book *At Peace in the Light*, "We have yet to realize that we are not poor, pitiful human beings trying to have a spiritual experience, but powerful spiritual beings trying to have a spiritual experience, and we have just not figured out how to do it yet." Also, Marianne Williamson put it more succinctly in her book *A Return to Love:* "We overvalue what we perceive with our physical senses, and we undervalue what we know to be true in our hearts." That is why many of us reject God or are afraid of God and afraid to love. That is why we often dismiss God from our thoughts and our lives and why we are afraid to give love unconditionally. We expect some passionate ecstasy—selfishly, for ourselves—a what's-in-it-for-me attitude.

Conversely, for me, because of the deep, unselfish love between Eileen and me, I was forced to explore more fully where my love was after she died, even though my traditional Christian faith told me that we were all saved by Jesus's crucifixion and resurrection. I realized this in a mildly intellectual and spiritual way. However, with the incomprehensible loss of my beloved, the depth of my despair was inconceivable and humanly impossible for me to accept. I had prayed every day of my wife's illness and coma, every day for a year, with all my heart, begging, pleading, crying for God to cure her. I prayed all the time, falling asleep exhausted in prayer, waking in prayer, almost throughout every minute of each day in prayer. I truly thought that somehow, some way, she would awake and all would be well again. I was in total denial that I would lose her. (I am even now in tears as I write and relive this most desolate time of my life.)

With her death, of course, I was physically and spiritually bankrupt. I truly wanted to die. Every day for months I asked God to kill me! Take me! Why was I here without her? Please let me die! Please, please just some way snuff out my life! Words cannot begin to express my loneliness, my emptiness, my pity for myself. Of course, God knew, and somewhere in the depth of my being, I knew that I had much to live for: our children, our grandchildren, two older sisters, some purpose yet in this life. "Thy will be done." However, during these first completely impossible weeks without her, I was a drag on everyone. My children carried me, instead of I helping them. I really don't know how I managed those first weeks and months.

It was at this time that my son, Nick, gave me some books to read by Elizabeth Kubler-Ross and another book entitled *We Don't Die* by Joel Martin and Patricia Romanowsky. The book *Hello From Heaven* by Bill and Judy Guggenheim also became a great help to me. During this period of overwhelming grief and anguish, I kept asking myself, asking my God, "Where is she? Where is my girl? Is she all right? Is there another life?" I couldn't accept anything less than she was alive, she was all right, she was happy, she could see us. Will I be with her someday? Yes, I believe, I told Him, but <u>SHOW ME!</u> I must know! Where is she? God, do you understand how much I love her, how much I miss her? Please tell me! I have to be with her someday and forever. Do you understand, my God? I BELIEVE You. But SHOW ME! How can I know?

I was a zombie. I continued to work every day, suppressing my grief and my emotions as best I could. When I was alone, I cried almost all the time. Except for the care and love of my children, I don't know how I lived. I have six adult children who have lives of their own, work and families. However, at least one of them was with me every day. My son Joe drove up from New York City, a two-hour drive, almost every night to have supper with me. He used to tease me that we would get to have dinner in every restaurant in Dutchess County. Nancy came up from Rye, New York to be with me every weekend. Eileen, who had recently finished college, stayed with me all summer. Theresa, who had moved next door to me, was with me each day, although as the mother of four children, she was quite busy. Jimmy built an addition to his house for me to live with him and his family. Nick, who lived in California, stayed on as long as he could, and when he had to go back, phoned me practically every day. They were all marvelous —a reflection of the love they received from their mother.

It was during this early and very trying period that wonderful and uplifting HAPPENINGS began to take place. We might call them coincidences, if you please. However, as result of my insights, I maintain that there are no coincidences. Everything has a purpose. Unbelievable wonders began to take place: my wife, through our God, giving me cause to heal, to understand, to believe. After-death communications, dream visions, improbable means of contact, became a reality. Slowly my faith grew. My heart knew and every fiber of my being awoke to the truth. The

A card and message from my son Nick's dear friend Adelaide captured so much:

"IN TIMES OF SORROW, LOVE HEALS."

Dear Dr. Ross,   3/28/96

I'm writing to tell you how sorry I am for your loss. Your wife - (and the marriage that you created with her and shared - Nick and I often talked about that at length) - has always

Thinking of you with special caring.

been one of my greatest influences. Her soft openness, quiet calm, and unconditional love and support for her family and those around her always touched and amazed me! I learned so much from her, and will always strive to follow her example.

You were blessed to have had her with you for so long. I'm so very, very sorry she was taken so soon.

Much Love & Prayers,
Adelaide

infinite love of my wife and me carried me to an unquestionable knowledge that there is more—much more—to come. Yes, you will be with her. Yes, you will know—because you will be transformed by your wisdom, faith, and unconditional love. Open your heart; look, listen, and receive.

Join me on my odyssey as I slowly began to understand some of the answers to those questions that had burned and ravished my very soul. My heart still anguishes constantly because she is not here, humanly with me. Many days I just burst out crying in my loneliness. However, I know she is with us, watches over us in ways we don't understand and can't comprehend in our human nature. More importantly, she is okay. She is joyful and at peace in a world we will understand and appreciate when we arrive there. Still, I tell her every day, "I can't wait to be with you. It's okay if I'm sad, my sweetest girl; I just miss you." And I know that some day I will be with her, forever.

It's just as George Anderson, the medium, said in the book *We Don't Die:*

"I want people to understand that life is everlasting. Everything that happens in your life has a purpose. There is no one you are close to who ever dies. Everyone just goes on to another stage of life that runs parallel to this one. Be at peace with yourself and fulfill your mission, knowing that your stay here is temporary and that you are doing something here to fulfill your spiritual purpose. Tune in more to yourself. And understand more within yourself so that you can find your way easier. Don't place too much emphasis on life materially. Place more emphasis on it spiritually. Death is not the end. It's the beginning. There is life everlasting. There is no such thing as death. That child, that husband, that wife, that loved one—they are still very much alive. It's just as if they've moved to Outer Mongolia and you may not see them again for many, many years."

So, am I just gullible, believing everything I read and hear, wanting so fervently and foolishly to believe that I have lost any semblance of reason, common sense, or intelligence just to make myself believe? To live in a fantasy land, just to survive my overwhelming loss? Emphatically no! I have not become a "crazy," a fanatic, a grief-stricken shell of a man. I did, however, become acutely aware of and open to many experiences, coincidences, happenings, occurrences, that forced me happily and luckily so to think, wonder, and explore what these extraordinary events mean to me. And, in the much broader sense, what they project in life and in the true meaning of living, creation, and God.

I am a plain and ordinary person, the guy next door. I have no special gifts or talents. I lived and still live a routine kind of life, and because I am human and imperfect, I have overwhelming feelings of loneliness and sadness. But now, I never despair or disbelieve.

Therefore, I would like to explain my transformation by telling you about ordinary and extraordinary people I have had the good fortune to know or to meet, who have aided me in my search for my wife.

I will start with the very first startling challenge to my intelligence, psyche, and wisdom. This challenge was presented to me from a dream by my cousin Sheila, which she had shortly after my Eileen died to this world.

CHAPTER
TWO

DREAMS HAVE CHANGED THE WORLD

"Six weeks after his death, my father appeared to me in a dream. It was an unforgettable experience and it forced me for the first time to think about Life after Death."
—*Carl G. Jung,*
from *Memories, Dreams, Reflections*

Dreams are an enigma. There are books, seminars, support groups, newspaper columns, all explaining dreams to help us in life situations. When we research and review all of this material, it simply comes down to what each of us individually makes of his or her own personal interpretation of this phenomenon. Most of the time we pay little or no attention to them, but once in a while a dream will impress itself upon our thoughts so firmly that we are forced to consider if something or someone is sending this dream experience specifically and especially to advise us on a decision or to change our life perspective in a very significant way. We have all had "impact" dreams which stir our emotions and intellect so intensely that we wonder, "What's it all about?" Is there some wisdom or purpose in that dream?

Many of the world's most celebrated people—scientists, doctors, authors, philosophers, religious—give credence to special dreams which have led them to their inspirations, decisions, and discoveries.

For example: Dante's *The Divine Comedy* might never have been published if not for a dream his son Jacopo had after his father's death. (Dante's sons had searched for months for parts of his manuscript and could not find the papers.) Dante came to his son Jacopo in a dream and was asked by Jacopo if he had completed the poem. Dante then showed his son a secret place in his room where the rest of his manuscript had been placed. The next day, Jacopo, with a lawyer friend, went to the room and found the papers as his dream indicated. Thus, the eventual publication of *The Divine Comedy* became a reality.

Billy Joel has been quoted in interviews as saying, "All of the music I have composed has come from a dream. I even dream arrangements and solos."

Mozart attributed some of his compositions to the music he heard in his dreams.

Niels Bohr claims his first concrete thoughts on "the quantum theory," for which he won a Nobel Prize, came to him in a dream.

Dreams are multi-cultural and cross all human barriers: age, sex, race, socio-economic status, and like music, are a universal language. Interpretation of dreams may, however, be influenced by cultural mores. Everyone dreams. Researchers believe that even animals dream. Have you ever noticed your pet while it is asleep, reacting to some invisible situation?

Dream research became more credible when, in 1958, rapid eye movement (R.E.M.) during sleep was found to be a common denominator of dreaming. Thus, the physiological phenomenon of dreaming through R.E.M. ushered in the academic and scientific study of dreams. The real excitement is, however, that dreaming, like other subconscious activity, is of great value individually and collectively. Dreams are healthy, informative, instructive, and creative. Even nightmares can be viewed as a wake-up call to listen and think.

Theories of dreaming are so diverse and numerous that it is safe to say we really don't know where dreams originate. Are all of our dreams manufactured in some special part of our brains, or do some dreams come from "outside" ourselves, so to speak, "telegraphed" from an external spiritual source? Certainly there are many anecdotal instances of precognitive, predictive, and premonitory dreams.

Dreams and dreaming can be categorized in many different ways. From my experience and from my understanding, dreams can be described simply as (1) Ordinary Dreams and (2) Big Dreams.

1. Ordinary Dreams

Most dreams are ordinary and seem to effect a frenzied, chaotic, murky (cloudy), disjointed, helter-skelter foundation, a sort of surrealistic chain of events. They are lacking in any reasonable orientation which, therefore, leads to a cartoonish, disconnected picture bouncing around in the subconscious sleep state. Included in this picture may be past and "future" experiences, known and unknown individuals, slipping in and out of this jumbled dream. Generally, most of this motion-picture dream is quickly forgotten when we awaken. However, if we take the time to review our dreams, we may realize some interesting and startling observations. For instance, I would like to describe a dream that I had this year, which, for me, involved closure of an incident that occurred when I was about 16 years old.

My father was the oldest of five brothers. They all got along pretty well, but at times one or the other of them would exhibit the explosive temper generally attributed to the Italian/Latin personality. One night I happened to overhear my father telling my mother that my Uncle Louie was getting on my father's nerves about some family situation. My father, however, was trying to keep calm about it and not "rock the boat." From the way he sounded, however, I perceived that my Dad was pretty irritated and dissatisfied with the way the situation was developing. (I now don't remember any particulars of the incident.) Somehow, at age 16, it seemed that I should defend my father, although he was fully capable of defending himself. I drove over to my Uncle Louie's house, swaggered in the front door calling loudly for him. I remember well that he was standing at the top of the stairs to the second floor, when I yelled to him in words to the effect that he had better leave my father alone and not give him any trouble. Of course, he became livid, and using a few choice words, ordered me out of his house. "You little so-and-so!" Well, I never heard anything more about that little caper from my father or my uncle.

Shortly thereafter, my uncle and his wife left the East Coast and moved to California, and there was little contact between our families. About 20 years later, while I was downtown and coming out of the local bank, I was surprised to see my Uncle Louie standing on the corner a few doors ahead of me. Our eyes met and I started toward him with the hope that the years had diffused our strained past relationship. However, he waved me away and turned and walked across the street. I never again saw my uncle alive. My father and all my uncles have long ago died and I am "the old guard" now.

During my life, I really experienced no guilt about the run-in with my Uncle Louie and it faded from my memory. However, this year I had a dream. It was kind of an "ordinary dream," mixed-up, chaotic, roving here and there and everywhere. However, one episode in this dream touched my heart, and on awakening caused me to sit up and take special notice of it. This episode of my night's dream involved me seeing many of my family, uncles, aunts, cousins, in a large garage planning some kind of picnic. We all went out to our cars to drive somewhere. Suddenly, I was back in the garage and my Uncle Louie was standing there with me. He smiled at me and gave me a big hug. I remember saying to him, "I want you to meet my wife, Eileen," fully realizing somehow that my Eileen was dead. With that, the dream sort of faded away, and that is all I remember about it. To my recollection, I never before dreamed about my Uncle Louie and did not carry any conscious burden of guilt about him. Therefore, how do I view this dream? Is it to be brushed aside as of little consequence, with no real meaning? Is it a jumbled, chaotic, mish-mash of a dream, a surrealistic bit of mumbo-jumbo, an insignificant subconscious memory from the past? Or, what is it? The meaning of this ordinary dream to me is now enormous. My Uncle Louie is impressing upon me that there is no bitterness in his heart any more. There is only love, which completely envelops everyone on the other side, when we will surely meet again, and all is right with the world. Thus goes the way of our frenzied, disorganized dreams— or are they?

2. Big Dreams

We are somewhat more than ourselves in sleep, and the slumber of the body seems to be but the waking of the soul.
—*Sir Thomas Browne*

Big dreams of our deceased loved ones are referred to as sleep-state ADC's (after-death communications) by researchers, and are definitely not chaotic or disorganized. They are totally clear and completely realistic to the experiencer. They are firm, orderly, vivid, colorful, purposeful, and insightful. Some of these dreams are "third party" dreams, when a loved one tells someone else something meant for you. Why this happens, we don't know. Maybe it is somehow easier for our loved one to contact this person than it is to reach us. Possibly this person is more intuitive or psychic than we are. Maybe our deceased loved one realizes it would be more believable to us coming from someone who is not so emotionally involved and deeply saddened as we are. Whatever the reason, this is exactly what happened in a dream to my second cousin, Sheila. This exciting, rejuvenating, and soul-searching communication from my Eileen through Sheila to me was one of the first impressive and welcome signs of my wife's continued existence in a special place which God has promised all of us.

I would like to tell you a little about my cousin. Sheila is a woman of great musical talent and ability, and also of integrity and uncanny intuition. She began to notice dreams of substance and meaning when she was about nine years old. One of the first dreams that she remembers was about a relative whom we will call Joan, who was hospitalized and in a coma during the time of this dream. In this dream, Joan was lying in the hospital bed and there was an open casket in the room. There was a very noticeable brightness around the casket and Sheila distinctly heard a voice say, "Joan, it is not your time," and the casket closed. Shortly thereafter, Joan did regain consciousness and recovered, living for many more years.

Sheila described these dreams as being extremely vivid, in color, and upon awakening she remembers exactly what took place. She now lives on the second floor of a house where her Aunt Nancy had lived before she died of cancer of the lung. While Nancy was alive, but in extremely poor medical condition, Sheila had a dream involving her grandmother, Nancy's mother, who had died years ago. In this dream, Grandmother Mary was sitting in the kitchen in a rocking chair where she generally sat. Mary was wearing an apron which Sheila recognized. Grandma told Sheila to sit down and said, "We are going to take your Aunt Nancy, you know, but everything is going to be all right." Nancy died shortly thereafter.

Sheila also described a dream which she had that proved to be of great assistance to her friend, Peggy. On a Friday and a Saturday night, Sheila had the exact same dream of a lady slumped over in a chair. She was dressed in a particularly striking brownish print dress. Sheila saw the lady leave her body and join thousands of other souls going toward a light. At the same time, Sheila's Aunt Nancy appeared and clearly said to her, "Support the one that is left and tell her that it was natural." On that Sunday, Sheila felt overwhelmed with emotion. After leading the church choir, she went home to rest quietly, even taking the telephone off the hook. The next day, Sheila's friend, Peggy, called and related that her mother-in-law had been found dead, slumped over in a chair in her apartment. Police and medical personnel investigated, judging that the woman had been dead about two days. Because the woman had been depressed about her own son-in-law's recent death, police speculated if she had taken her own life. However, no autopsy had been authorized to verify any of these speculations, and this left Peggy even more unnerved and grief-stricken about the death.

Sheila attended the wake and recognized Peggy's mother-in-law, whom she had never seen before, as the lady in her dream. Even more startling is the fact that she was wearing the same brownish print dress that she had been wearing during Sheila's dream. Sheila talked to Peggy about the dream and stressed to her that Sheila's deceased Aunt Nancy said that the death was natural and not self-induced. Of course, this knowledge from Sheila was a great relief for

Peggy and gave her the added strength she needed in her time of sorrow.

But now, let me relate to you the most important dream of my life, one that didn't even come to me directly. This special dream was a "third-party" dream that came to Sheila less than a month after Eileen died. With this dream, there occurred a number of other very exciting, significant, enlightening, and truly beautiful gifts that were presented to me by my deceased wife through a loving and compassionate God. Before I introduce this very "big dream," let me ask you to consider some perplexing questions. Why did my wife, Eileen, appear to my cousin Sheila instead of to my sister or daughter-in-law, who have had, what I believe, are very specific after-death communications? Was Sheila so concerned about my grief that she consciously or subconsciously wanted to give me relief? Wouldn't my sister or daughter-in-law see and experience even more closely my very intense and numbing feelings? Why didn't my perfect love Eileen come directly to me? Does Sheila have a more powerful intuition than I do? Certainly she had had many curious and psychic experiences throughout her life, and maybe my Eileen wanted to be sure I got her message. Possibly since my Eileen had newly-arrived "over there," she was not able to achieve this communication without help. As you will see, Sheila's Aunt Nancy, my cousin, accompanied Eileen on this journey. Is all of this pure balderdash? Well, decide for yourself. Of course, you must have a heart that is open to the truths of a connected universe through God's unconditional love and mercy for all of us.

After this dream occurred, Sheila, who has a very demanding schedule, planned to call me, however, she didn't immediately get to it. One day while she was shopping she met my sister, and after they greeted each other, she said, "Tell cousin Joe to call me, as I have something important to tell him." Since Sheila had said it was important, I telephoned her at my first opportunity. But our schedules were really tight and Sheila said, "I have to tell you now, and maybe we can meet some other time to discuss it." And then she said, "I saw Eileen in a dream and she was RADIANT!" I was bowled over. I really had to catch my breath. She continued, "Aunt Nancy came to me in a dream, but she stepped aside and pointed to someone else who appeared to be floating just above the foot of my bed. It was Eileen! My eyes gazed from her feet to her head. She was wearing a long white gown which was tight around the waist and spread out in a wide circle downward. It was scalloped at the bottom, with the edges shining in a bright, golden appearance. As I looked at her, her hands were folded in front, and she had such a peaceful and beautiful smile. She was simply glowing and there was a brightness emanating from the area all around her. Eileen said to me, " *Tell him not to be depressed. I'm in a better place than I was before.* " Sheila went on, "I was so surprised and wanted to talk to her, when I suddenly awoke. Cousin Joe, she looked so happy and wonderful." I was totally and completely amazed and didn't know what to think or say, but I instantly, to the depths of my being, knew that my dearest love in the whole world had found a way to communicate with me. I believed immediately in my heart and soul the universal truth: We don't die! I will be with her again and forever.

Of course, you would have to know my Eileen to understand that this is exactly how she would report such an astounding revelation, for she did not exaggerate or overplay anything. She just "told it like it was" and you knew you could believe her. She wouldn't say, for instance, "Tell him I love him." That would be too personal. Or, "Tell him how wonderful it is here." Rather, "Tell him it's okay and not to worry." That's exactly the way my sweetest love would come to me. It is now six years later and this spiritually overpowering conversation with Sheila is deeply impressed in my heart. The truth of it is no less, and when I am sad and overwhelmed with missing my special Eileen, I say to myself, *"Tell him not to be depressed. I'm in a better place than I was before."*

I must digress here about Sheila's quotation, "I saw Eileen in a dream and she was RADIANT." Webster's unabridged dictionary states, "Radiant. Emitting rays of light, shining, bright, bright with joy." When I think of someone described as radiant, I picture rays of light projecting from them as with saints, heroes, angels, and God, the most radiant light of all. This kind of radiance gives me a feeling of reverence and awe. My radiant Eileen is one of God's special and holy people. Therefore, I repeat, this event was one of the most wondrous, exciting, and compelling experiences of my life.

What I call the "truth and wisdom" of God in our world is found by many of us who see Him in all phases of life, whether it is pain and suffering or joy and love. Therefore I would like to describe other instances of the use of the word "radiant" which I found in my research.

This next dream, from the book *Messengers* by Patricia Treece, involves two nuns who were also true sisters and lived during the late 19th century. They were from the same order, but lived far apart in different communities. Sister Mary died on May 14, 1880. That evening, a priest received a telegram with the sad news at the community of the other sister-nun, Sister Felicina. It was his duty to inform Sister Felicina of her older sister's death. He was very nervous, as he knew of the great love the two sisters had for each other. However, when he arrived at Sister Felicina's residence, he was immediately surprised, as she said to him, "Father, last night I had the most wonderful dream. Yet, somehow it wasn't a dream, it was so real. I really saw my sister. She was clothed in a splendid white light. She was RADIANT. She smiled at me and said, 'Good-bye, Felicina. Good-bye.'" Then Felicina added, "I wonder what all that means?" Of

Sheila's
Dream
Vision

course, that made the message to Sister Felicina a much easier task.

Here is another dream echoing the beauty of radiance from the book *Hello From Heaven* by Bill and Judy Guggenheim. In this dream, a young schoolteacher heard from her close friend, Gary. She lived in Chicago, and he was a graduate student in a city 250 miles away. This young woman, Debbie describes a very vivid dream in which Gary came and sat on the edge of her bed. He was extremely happy and at peace. He was in the best health ever, looking very RADIANT. A glow of white surrounded him. Among other things, he said to her, "No matter what happens, you have to go on because you're on the right path." Debbie was troubled by this dream because she didn't know what it meant. That evening while preparing supper she had the TV news on. Startling and numbing news gripped her. Gary had been killed the night before in a terrible car accident.

Many such dream experiences have been recounted from all over the world during all periods of history and from people from all walks of life. Are these life experiences inconsequential, valueless, and meaningless? Absolutely not! The wisdom and truth of the universe has always been recognized by many people of faith and integrity.

This next experience from *Messengers* involves a philosopher professor, Jacques Maritain, who at one time taught at Princeton University and was known for his forthrightness and integrity. His sister-in-law, Vera, lived with Maritain and his wife and took over running the house for them. She became a victim of cancer. Maritain reported that on April 10, 1959, Vera had "a dream or vision." In this dream her dead father appeared "RADIANT with youth and with light." She asked him if he had come to take her and he said, "Not yet." In December of that year, she died peacefully at home, and her last intelligible word was "Papa."

I have fallen in love with the word RADIANT. It now

inspires me with the knowledge and anticipation that I will join my beloved Eileen in a world resplendent with beauty and joy.

I would like to close this chapter with some dreams which occurred centuries apart.

There lived a famous author and statesman during the time 100-50 years BC. His name was Marcus Tullius Cicero and he related the following dream in his well-known essay *On Divination:*

Two companions were traveling together and when evening came they decided to rest for the night. One stayed at the local inn and the other stayed at the house of a friend. During the night, the traveler who was staying at his friend's house had this disturbing dream: His friend came to him and said, "I have been murdered by the innkeeper and thrown into a cart and covered with dung. Please come to the gate very early and avenge my death." So in turmoil and upset by the dream was the other, that he did go to the inn very early and found a worker just about to drive away with the cart. Confronted there, the driver ran away and the body was retrieved. The innkeeper was reported to the authorities and received due punishment.

Thousands of years after Marcus Tullius Cicero's dream, my youngest daughter, Eileen, who was named after her mother, told me of this dream which she clearly remembers almost six years after her Mom died.

In her dream, she was finishing college and told me, "I came out of my classroom and looked down the hallway. Mom was standing there. She was wearing a plain brown dress which I did not recognize. I ran down the hall and threw my arms around her, thinking, 'But she is dead.' Mom hugged me but didn't say anything. There were people walking up the hallway to my left, but I know they didn't see her. I felt so good. I wanted to talk to her, but I suddenly awoke."

My oldest daughter, Theresa, told me of her heartening, but also sad dream:

After watching my mom become sick, suffer, slowly disappear, and then finally die, I thought I would never—and I mean never—be the same. I was right about that. The void and pain from the loss of my mom is an ever-present reality that I contend with every day. But the intense love and bond that I had with my mom has continued. Our relationship is very real and I still draw so much strength and comfort from her. I know it sounds very contradictory: an immense pain and void *and* love and comfort. Believe, me, I get confused, frustrated, sad, and baffled by my conflicting feelings and emotions all the time. I hate not having my Mom's physical, human, touchable, beautiful presence here with me. But I love the soft and gentle way she still touches my heart and mind in her spiritual existence. I am a firm believer that we are all blessed with a never-ending life, first here on Earth and then a much more complex and joyful life in Heaven with God and our loved ones. I have felt this to be true ever since I can remember. That knowledge and firm belief is a true gift from God. He has somehow entered my heart and mind in such a way that I just simply have no doubt about it. And I have no doubt that my mom has found ways of keeping up our relationships. I have always felt that one way the people we love can say "hello" is while we are asleep. I use the term asleep because I think the term "dream" leads one to thinking of something that is not a reality, that it is one's own mind and thoughts being played out. When someone, in my humble opinion, reaches out to us while we're sleeping, it is a whole different feeling and venue than our dreams. I have "dreamed" about the people I love many times, but only a few times have the people I love used my time while sleeping to be with me. My mom has done this for me two times. Each time, I have been completely aware that I was <u>not</u> dreaming, but that I was having a communication on a very personal level. The first time was a simple, brief encounter. I was sitting on my bed and my mom was sitting next to me. She was holding my hand and smiling at me. I was so happy to see her; I could hardly believe that I was this blessed. She called me "Sweetie" and told me she loved me. Then she told me she wanted me to give her clothes, especially her winter coat, to my Aunt Ann, her sister. I knew exactly the coat she was talking about and told her I would be sure to give it to Aunt Ann. We sat for a few minutes together and then she said she had to go. I didn't want her to go and I started crying. I awakened crying, but also very happy to have had that time with my mom. I called my Aunt Ann that day and told her my mom wanted her to have her coat! I think my Mom knows how hard it is for me to be parted from her in this way. A few months later, my Mom paid me another visit. We were walking through a big, circular house with many windows and a fountain in the middle. My sister Nancy was with us. Nancy and I were just spending time with my mom. She was trying to explain to us that she needed to go, to be away from us on Earth, and that she knew this was hard for us to accept. She was trying to help us with it, but I was very sad and didn't want to let go of her hand. I know it was hard for her to have to leave me like that. I realized if she left, it must be the right and best thing for her to do. I still couldn't help but be upset and not want to be without her in this world. The fact that she took the time to try and help me means a lot and I do draw comfort from that and try to be more accepting of it. Although, I must admit, I don't do so well some of the time. I do think I have a truer sense of trust about my mom being where she needs to be and still caring about all of us. These visits from my mom were simple and short, but very loving and important to me. They have had a big impact on my heart. I have an even stronger faith in my mom and how she watches over us, even though I still wish she was right next to me with her hand on mine.

Surely, a dream is just a dream—no more and no less— just a part of the sleep process. Or what? You decide. As for me, my eternal love spoke to me through a dream. I believe. God does not deceive.

CHAPTER
THREE

I KNOW IT WAS SHE

"It is presumption in us when the help of heaven we count the act of men."
— William Shakespeare

"Evidence of seemingly paranormal goings-on come in from all over—from many different fields, from many different belief systems and from all corners of the world..."
— Bernard Gittelson,
Intangible Evidence

When I was a kid, probably just old enough to understand some things, my Great Aunt Julia died. She was very ill, and in those days people were treated at home more often than in the hospital. This story about Great Aunt Julia is told over and over again as part of our family lore. Her children and siblings were keeping a daily vigil when one day, she suddenly sat up in bed and said, "I see Gaetano (her husband)," as she pointed across the room. "He's coming for me." Then she lay back down in bed. Shortly thereafter, Aunt Julia took her last breath, and I presume, went happily to join Gaetano.

These stories were not uncommon from our ancestors, but, of course, as our society has become more sophisticated, we have had no use for such foolishness. It is not surprising to me, however, that thousands of after-death communications are coming to the fore. Many of them are so factual and evidential that it is simply foolhardy to deny their existence.

I have my own happenings from my little corner of the world. Here they are!

My grandson, Joe IV, was born on April 17, 1996, not quite a month after my wonderful Eileen had died on March 20, 1996. Shortly after his birth he developed severe respiratory problems and had to be admitted to a special pediatric hospital for treatment. My son Joe and my daughter-in-law Mary Beth spent all their time at the hospital, as you can well understand their anxiety. Finally Joe convinced Mary Beth to go home for a short rest and then to come back to the hospital. He said that he would do the same when she returned.

What occurred when she was home is the second of my most extraordinary happenings. It filled me with joy and hope, increasing my thoughts and beliefs in that which I already knew. We are eternal beings! Although my "intellect" and "reason" kept fighting me and kept pressing doubt into my heart and mind, my soul began to grasp the truth: we *are* eternal beings!

To understand this powerful event, you need to know that Mary Beth is blessed with an intuitive awareness that is well above the normal realm. Most of us have some grasp of intuitive awareness. Here are some common examples. (1) You are seated in a restaurant or a theater when you suddenly have the feeling "someone is staring at me!" You know, no doubt, that it is true. As you casually gaze around the area, that someone casually looks away, someone you don't even know. (2) The telephone rings at home and you absolutely know who is calling; no reason to know, but you do. And what is more interesting, you are right. (3) You are walking down the street and it is not a particularly crowded way. Suddenly you get a chill and the hair bristles at the back of your neck. Someone is directly behind you and quickly walks on past you. You didn't see or hear anything, but your "feeling" was uncannily accurate. That is intuition. Some call it our sixth sense, for without seeing, hearing, smelling, touching, or tasting, we absolutely know. We have that "gut feeling." Intuition at its highest awareness gives us our greatest and most wonderful experiences.

Well, to get back to my story, Mary Beth went home from the hospital as Joe suggested. She was very unsettled, tired, and worried, and decided to take a calming shower. What happened next is not an unusual experience, having happened to literally thousands of people in this mysterious world of ours. Mary Beth told me that while she was taking her shower, "I could feel Mom's presence. I know she was there with me. I had to smile that Mom was there during my shower. You know what a private person Mom was. I could hear her voice inside my head saying, 'It's going to be all right.' And just as quickly as she had arrived, she had gone." I questioned Mary Beth about this "sentient" experience (as they are referred to by parapsychologists) because it touched me so deeply that I wanted to be sure of all the details.

"Yes, Dad, I just felt her presence. Yes, she was really there. It was Mom. I could just feel her presence. I didn't see her, but it was Mom."

"What about hearing her?"

"I could hear her voice. It was definitely Mom's voice. I heard it in my head, not through my ears. No, it was not telepathy. It was really Mom's voice."

I can definitely tell you that Mary Beth is a very stable

individual. She is a matter-of-fact, down-to-earth person. She is not flighty or easily influenced. She has the exact persona for a "prove it to me" journalist/TV producer, which she is.

I have heard and read about many such sentient experiences in my research, but none of them were more poignant to me than this experience of Mary Beth. Now, with Sheila's dream and this unexpected experience, the foundation of my pyramid of faith was beginning to take shape.

In fact, in my little world of Dutchess County, New York, many such experiences have been related to me. None of the people who have told me of their "happenings" are looking for their "fifteen minutes of fame." Actually, having heard me talk about such things, as I often do, they would mention that they or their mother, aunt, father, etc. had the same thing happen to them. I would have to pursue the conversation and investigate the happening gently and carefully to hear many wonderful and spiritually exciting experiences.

Talk about not knowing things...I did not even know what went on in my own backyard. My oldest sister, Nancy, who is very well known in this area as a caring and exceptional teacher, finally told me of her experience after hearing about Mary Beth's experience.

Our mother died at the age of 96 in the year 1992. Two years later, my sister Nancy was diagnosed with cancer of the colon. Her doctors were fairly well-convinced by their many tests that it was an operable cancer and there would be a good chance for a cure. As I look back now, they were correct, as Nancy is alive and well.

Nancy said to me that our mom had come to her a few days after the operation. Mom didn't say anything, but, "I felt she was definitely there in my hospital room." As I questioned Nancy, she related the following experience:

It was about three or four days after the surgery and Nancy was feeling a little more comfortable. All of a sudden, she felt Mom's presence in the room! Nancy was totally shocked and said, "Mom, what are you doing here?" Internally, "You're dead!" When she described it to me, Nancy said, "I know she was there. I didn't see her and she didn't say anything, but I just got the feeling she was there to comfort me. It was a very intense presence, very strong. It was really Mom. I was very startled and surprised, and after I went into the corridor looking for her, she just disappeared. Her presence was gone." If you knew my sister Nancy, you would understand that when she uses words like "intense" and "strong," she is very serious. She is not one to fabricate her feelings.

Wow! All I read about sentient ADC's is hitting me smack in the head. These things are right here in my own alley.

Before I describe Mary Beth's second sentient experience, let me tell you of some evidentiary ADC's related to me by Betty, a financial secretary friend of mine, involving a combination of paranormal events.

When Betty was eight years old, her father became very sick with cancer. At that time, Betty's mother decided to send Betty to stay with her grandparents. Her mother wanted to give more time and care to her husband. One evening, when Betty was out on the back porch with her grandparents, she suddenly saw a "new star" in the sky. A strange feeling came over her and she said to her grandparents, "My Daddy just died. I see a new star in the sky." Her grandparents were, of course, surprised and disturbed and tried to comfort her that Daddy was sick, but had not died. Betty repeated, "No. My Daddy just died." It was 8:20 p.m. The next morning, Betty's uncle came to the house and told them that her father had died the night before. The time he died was 8:20 p.m.

Betty described another incident in her family that happened to her niece, Carol. Carol fell asleep while driving her car and had a head-on collision with another car. Carol was killed in the accident. Before anyone had heard of the accident, three people in the family received separate messages making them aware of the tragedy. One was Carol's grandmother, who had a dream at that time. In this dream, Carol came to her grandmother and said, "Grandma, I'm okay and I'm very happy." Carol also appeared to her sister-in-law who was awake at home, and with whom she had a very close relationship. Carol appeared in a kind of mist, but very clearly it was Carol, and again, she said, "I'm okay and I'm very happy," and then she just disappeared.

At the same time, Carol's sister was celebrating her 18th birthday at a restaurant with friends. All of the sudden her sister had this strange and obsessive feeling. She had to leave the restaurant and go home. When she arrived home, she received a telephone call informing her of Carol's death in the accident.

These different incidents introduce other types of ADCs that have been described, some in great detail, in the literature. Again, they are right here in our own little community. Now, back to my daughter-in-law's other beautiful ADC experience.

Baby Joe did recover from his respiratory problems and was able to go home, much to the joy of his parents.

Mary Beth related a second sentient ADC which happened two-to-three weeks after Joe IV was brought home from the hospital. Mary Beth was in her bedroom sitting on the bed and had Joe lying on his back in the middle of the bed. Suddenly, Mary Beth felt Mom's (my Eileen's) presence in the bedroom. She was definitely there, and even the baby seemed to have an awareness of it. Again, Mary Beth did not see Mom, but she knew without a doubt that Mom was there. Mom said to Mary Beth in her head, "He's so cute."

Mom's presence was evident for about half a minute and then she disappeared.

These experiences of Eileen's presence that Mary Beth felt were not her only such experiences. Mary Beth's father had died of a heart condition when she was in her teens. She has had some exciting sentient experiences from him. One she related to me is the kind that has occurred with many loved ones when there seemed to be a difficult situation developing. They are generally refereed to as "crisis experiences."

Mary Beth was driving alongside the Charles River in Boston during a severe thunderstorm. The car began to skid in the heavy rain. Suddenly, her father's presence was there telling her how to turn out of the skids and giving her confidence and encouragement. Needless to say, Mary Beth began to relax a little and felt quite relieved with her father's presence helping to navigate in the storm.

This next ADC was told to me by Brian, a good friend of mine, who is also a close friend of Ken, to whom this ADC happened. Ken was driving from Washington, D.C. to Providence, Rhode Island on a Sunday night. He was returning to work after a pleasant weekend visit at home with his mother and some friends. Ken got a very late start from D.C. after that pleasant weekend at home and was a little tired and sleepy as he drove along the highway. He began to doze off and his head started to bob. At that very instant, someone tapped him on the shoulder from the back seat. He was quite surprised, since no one was with him. As he took a quick look in the back of the car, he saw his father sitting there. (Dad had died years before.) He had to be dreaming! As Ken drove a little farther along the road, again he began to doze off and his head began to droop. Again, there was an unmistakable tap on his shoulder and a quick backward glance revealed his father sitting there in the back seat. This scenario repeated itself a number of times until

Ken had just about reached his destination. Ken's father appeared with a tapping just when Ken needed him and was falling off asleep. Then Dad was gone. Ken, who is a perfectly realistic and normal young man, is convinced that his father was with him on that trip in divine ways which are unexplainable, but nonetheless are absolutely true and wonderful.

About a month after Eileen died, our family suffered an even more startling and heart-rending tragedy. My wife's foster brother, who with his family lived about 30 miles north of us, was with three of his children in the upstairs bedroom of his house. It was a very old wooden house. Suddenly, unexpected circumstances occurred in the living room of the house sparking a fire which in a flash enveloped the whole house. John and three of his children were trapped in the upstairs bedroom and died there. This overwhelming accident caused an indescribable amount of suffering to our large family. John was about 12 years younger than my wife Eileen, and they were so very close that he loved her like a second mother.

Our family gathered at my home for the wake. The kitchen has a large picture window which faces the front of the house. A semicircular driveway leads to the road. It is directly in front of the kitchen window. Mary Beth stayed at home that evening with the children while the rest of us went to the funeral home. She was alone in the kitchen and happened to look out of the picture window. Standing in the driveway, in a physical state, was John and two of his children, one on each side of him. He was definitely there, looking into the house. Then they slowly drifted upward and away.

Mary Beth has no doubt about what she saw at that moment. How to explain it? Who can? Hundreds of people have similar experiences. Are they all hallucinating or in some unbalanced psychological state? I think not. For instance, did Carol's sister-in-law, described previously, hallucinate her experience when she did not even know that Carol had been in an accident and died?

In the literature, there are numerous and diverse ADC's reviewed from all over the world. How they occur, and what they mean, is for each one of us to decide in the depth of our own heart and soul, with complete integrity and sincerity.

I have described dream visions, sentient experiences, and visual experiences from intimate local accounts. These and many more that I will relate (some beautiful things that came only to me) are the beginning of God's way, I believe, of answering positively my constant tears and anguish, bolstering the truth of my faith.

Here is an experience of another young man who also played basketball for a Division I college. Coincidentally, I delivered him 31 years ago while I was a practicing obstetrician. This happened a number of years ago when Brian was visiting his parents in Alaska. It was during this time that a friend of his with whom he had played basketball in high school died after having a serious accident. Brian was at home resting on his parents' bed. He was not asleep, although he was very relaxed and comfortable. Suddenly his high school friend appeared at the foot of the bed. He looked very calm, standing about six inches off the floor, and although he was not rock solid, he was perfectly clear to Brian. Brian was startled, almost mesmerized by the vision, which lasted about 15 to 20 seconds. There was no communication, but Brian had the feeling that his friend was showing Brian that he was all right. This experience for Brian, to say the least, was extraordinary, but as he related it to me, was "definitely very real."

I often reflect on an ADC that happened to Thomas Merton before he became history's most famous Trappist monk at the Abbey of Gethsemani in Kentucky. This happened many years before he wrote his famous, heartwarming autobiography *The Seven Story Mountain.* Thomas Merton was in his teens at the time and was traveling through Italy visiting historic areas and churches in Rome. His father had died in 1931 when Tom was 16 and this trip was not long after the death of his father. One night, when he was in his hotel room, Tom had the sudden and overwhelming feeling that his father was present there with him. It was a most definite and very strong personal feeling. This experience and some other personal revelations were helpful in leading him to a life of spirituality.

A similar experience occurred to Edith Stein, the brilliant, thoughtful, and well-known doctor of philosophy. She was from a very devout Jewish family of Germany. After much soul-searching and meditation and after reading the autobiography of St. Teresa of Avila, almost accidentally, as the book fell off a shelf and landed right in front of her, Edith Stein, at the age of 31, decided to convert to Catholicism and was baptized on January 1, 1922. Then in October of 1933, after continued study and discussion, this worldly professor was stirred to give herself completely to the contemplative and prayerful life of a Carmelite nun.

Ironically, this was about the same time that Hitler took over power in Germany and thus began one of the most infamous periods of world history. This was the time when he fostered his inhuman hate advanced by his anti-Semitic, anti-racial, anti-Catholic, anti-Gypsy, homophobic treatment of anyone or anything in Germany that was "non-Aryan." Thousands of victims were herded into prisons and gas chambers and slaughtered at the hands of the Nazis. It so happened that on September 14, 1936, Edith Stein, now Sister Teresa Benedicta, was renewing her vows. After the ceremony, Sister Benedicta told another nun, "When my turn came for the renewal, my mother was with me. I distinctly felt her presence." Later that day, a telegram arrived from home at Breslan announcing the death of her mother.

She had died at the very hour when Sister Benedicta had renewed her vows; thus another sentient ADC was recorded for posterity.

On August 2, 1942, Sister Teresa Benedicta, with thousands of other prisoners, including her sister Rosa, who had also joined the Carmelite order, were arrested and transported to the Auschwitz prison. On August 7, 1942, they were herded into the gas chamber and had their lives snuffed out by an inhuman Nazi regime. Little did these Nazis realize that a better life awaited their victims. Sister Teresa rejoined her mother in the infinite love and joy of the other world that awaits all of us.

My Eileen died on March 20, 1996, and in the month of June I moved from our big house to the little cottage that was on our property about 50 feet from the big house. My daughter Theresa, her husband Jim, and their four children moved into the main house. The cottage has two small bedrooms, a bathroom, a living room, and a kitchen. My sister-in-law Ann used to live in the cottage. Besides being sisters, she and my Eileen were close friends.

Sometime in July, Joe, Mary Beth, and baby Joe came to visit me on a weekend. We fixed it so that they all could sleep in the living room, as the bedrooms were too small for the three of them. It was that Sunday morning when Mary Beth told me that Mom, my Eileen, had been there. It was about 3 a.m. when Mary Beth awoke to check on Joe IV and immediately sensed Mom's presence around the crib. It was very powerful and uplifting. However, Mom did not say anything at that time. My Eileen had definitely been there during the early morning, and although I did not sense it, I felt very excited about Mary Beth's sentient experience. Was God allowing Eileen to help us during the time of our sorrow and grief? Yes, I believe so.

Many more unexplainable ADC's have occurred for me and for my friend Kim, as well, since the tragic loss of her husband Dan. Some of the most difficult circumstances arise when one partner of a young couple who have children suddenly collapses and dies without any warning. Such a tragic circumstance involves Kim, who lost a loving and caring husband from a heart attack in the fullness of his life at the age of 37. As the medical examiner who investigated this case, I spoke to Kim shortly after her husband's death, trying to console her. I started to tell her about my belief that my wife was still alive in the next world when she interrupted me and said, "I believe that. Dan has already been here." Then she went on to tell me, "The first night I was sitting on the couch very sad and crying when suddenly I got this tingling sensation in my body. It felt very strange, very strange, and then I began to feel very relaxed. He was right there with me. I know it, and I felt very relaxed and at peace."

I spoke with Kim a number of times. She related two dreams that she had. But were they? Kim went on, "I lay on the floor. I wasn't feeling very well and I was just falling asleep, half-asleep, when I had this dream. Dan was standing in the kitchen facing me with his shoulders halfway into the hallway, and he said, 'Did you ever think it would be like this?' It was so real, so intense, and the adrenaline began to flow, and I was instantly awake. That's how real it was.

Kim described another short dream to me. "Dan was sitting in the bowling alley and I came up to him. He looked up to me and said, 'I'm okay.' Then he put his hand on my shoulder.

After Dan died, Kim's brother moved in with her and the family. Kim then related to me how her husband didn't like the heat. "He would be just as happy sleeping out in the snow." Kim and her brother were sitting in the living room. This was before she changed the rug where Dan had collapsed, since they were unable to remove the spots of blood where he had lain. Her brother happened to touch the rug and looked at her very quizzically and asked her to touch the spot. It was very cold to them. The rest of the rug was not cold.

Kim also described an experience she had relating to her husband's penchant for the cold. "I know it was Dan. I was sitting in bed doing cross stitching and talking out loud to him when the lights flickered. The lights never flickered. Then I felt like he put his hand on my neck, and it was ice cold. Then it went away. It wasn't a shiver. It was a really cold spot. I know it was Dan."

This next ADC comes from Penny Breda, a teacher's helper and mother of unquestioned integrity. Here are Penny's exact words to me.

It was in 1974. My grandmother was in Richfield and she had been bedridden for a few years. She very much wanted to die. She had a lot of faith and she was tired of lying in bed and being taken care of and being a burden. I believe she was 87. So, my children were in Baltimore and my husband and I went over to Richfield to have Thanksgiving with my Mom and my grandmother. I went in and spoke to her for a few minutes, but she didn't respond back much.

I went home and I was thinking. "Boy, it would really be nice if she would get her wish and she would die." The next morning I got a phone call that she had passed away about five in the morning. At six in the morning they had taken the body out of the house. It was my mother who called. My mother was not terribly upset because my mother and my grandmother were not very close. My mother's main concern at that time was that we come over to Richfield and help her go to the bank. (She had a polio leg.) So I went over with my husband. My mother was getting dressed and I was sitting on my grandmother's couch, a little two-seater where she always sat in front of the fireplace.

I don't think I was even thinking much of anything, but, suddenly my grandmother was talking to me! I can't tell you if it was audible by ear or if it was just in my head. No one else was in the room with me. <u>And she said</u>, 'I want you to let your mother know I'm all right. I'm in a wonderful place and I'm happy and she shouldn't worry about me.' And that was it! And, I mean, I was totally startled, and it actually felt like this communication was coming from somewhere up in here (putting her arms outward and upward in front of her), except that I was so amazed that I didn't look. I wasn't looking for ways to describe it. I was just totally WOW! And I didn't even tell anyone for three months because I thought they'd think I was so grief-stricken, they'd have to send me to the psychiatrist for this kind of thing. So I just didn't say anything, and I didn't tell my mother, either. Which means, I didn't deliver the message. I told my husband three months later. I never did tell my mother.

I said, "May I ask you one thing? When you heard this voice, did you hear her *voice?*"

"It was her voice, and I think she said my name. But it was her voice; it was my grandmother. She was talking to me. But I was so happy, you know, not because I was worried about her, because I said, 'WOW! Who would ever believe it?' But now, I know what other people don't know and may never know. But I know!"

Penny was very animated at this time. Then she said to me, "My father died when I was 11. I spent a lot of time thinking about him, but I never felt him around."

There are some ADC's which have what I like to call "special effects." There are different kinds of "special effects," but some of the best involve a deceased relative or friend leaving something solid behind as a gift or a token of their love. Such ADC's have been described by people of sound mind and good character throughout history.

Before I tell you about an amazing local occurrence which was told to me by one of my secretaries, let me describe some wonderful happenings from my research and reading.

This ADC is described by astrophysicist Michael Shallis in his exceptional book *The Electric Connection*. He tells about some people who have many allergies and a serious sensitivity to electricity. Some of these people also have a psychic element to their personalities. He describes a young, happily married mother who is a victim of all of the above as well as having psychic ability. She has seen auras around some people and has seen two apparitions. One of these was of her deceased grandmother who left her old hairnet as a token of her visit.

From the very powerful and compelling book *Messengers—After-Death Appearances of Saints and Mystics* by Patricia Treece, comes this! The short version is: A well-known person in a Pennsylvania hospital was dying of acute and chronic bleeding due to his severe alcoholism. Very late one evening, an elderly white-robed nun entered the room. She smoothed the sheets and plumped up his pillow and told him he would not die since he "had too much work to do." The next morning the doctor came and checked him, saying, "I don't know what happened, Jack, but your bleeding has stopped." He walked out of the room shaking his head in disbelief. The nurses were also amazed and wondered where he got the green scapular pinned to the shoulder of his gown. He told them that the old nun—describing her to them—must have pinned it on him last night. The nurses said that was impossible. No old nun was on the floor last night. He said the nun probably slipped by when they weren't looking. The nurses smiled and said the nun he described had been dead for several years. He must have dreamed it. Well, Jack still has the green scapular to prove it. He recovered and has been well and sober for many years, now counseling other alcoholics. He is still a well-known personality in that area of Pennsylvania.

And now I would like to report one of the most interesting, heartwarming, and mind-boggling experiences I have ever heard or read about in my few years of research.

This ADC occurred during World War II, a time that I remember as almost like a second war for independence. There was so much love and faith and camaraderie at that time. We all had one goal: to save America and the world! We worked together, cared for each other, and respected each other.

It was at this time of incongruity that a young man went off to war. It wasn't too long after that, like so many other young and brave men, he was killed in action. Joanne, who is one of my secretaries, tells me that this young man and his sister, Joanne's mother, were very close, very loving, and caring of each other. The young man's body was sent home for his funeral. He was laid-out in his captain's dress uniform. Joanne's mother was overwhelmed with grief.

Within a week after the funeral, she awakened one night and somehow was compelled to get out of bed and go into the living room. As she sat in a chair, her special captain brother appeared to her. He said to her, "I am all right. I love you and someday we will all be together."

At that time her husband noticed that she was not in bed and becoming concerned, he went into the living room and found her alone sitting in a chair. Her fist was clenched tightly around something and it took some effort to open her hand. There to his surprise and bewilderment was the captain's bars of her brother. Joanne has seen these same captain's bars. Joanne's mom swore to a very skeptical husband that she had never had any captain's bars from her brother until that very night.

I leave you with this quote from a cartoon in the New York *Daily News:* "Only a fool believes in the word 'impossible.'"

CHAPTER
FOUR

THERE ARE NO COINCIDENCES

"No pessimist ever discovered
the secrets of the stars,
or sailed to an uncharted
land, or opened a new
heaven to the human spirit."

—*Helen Keller*

This next chapter is one of the most important and significant chapters in this book and of my life. These deeply compelling events that follow enriched my faith and repeatedly filled my heart with the irrevocable truth and wisdom of an eternal connection with my wife Eileen. In these exciting synchronicities (I think of them as small miracles), the reality of our continuity in a universal plan of our God of Love has been imprinted on my soul, and, I have found, also on the souls of many others by their own perceptive happenings.

I know of this exquisitely beautiful and perfect love through 39 years of the gift of joy in my life from my special

45

girl. We needed only to be together to be supremely happy and contented. We lived together in another dimension within ourselves—a perfect world—wherever we were, whatever we were doing. As Eileen said to me in a card which I always carry with me:

I miss you
Even when you're
Only away for
A little while.

—Eileen

My sister-in-law Ann tells me, "You two were on your honeymoon all of your lives." Therefore, I know Eileen was allowed to reach me after her death by means that I would understand, grasp, and value during these overwhelmingly impossible human years without her.

The first wonders that gave me the courage and will to continue in this life have been described by her appearance in Sheila's dream: "Tell him I am in a better place than I was before." And, by her four sentient appearances to my daughter-in-law: "Yes, Dad, I know she was here. I have heard her voice. Yes, it was definitely Mom."

However, these next experiences, outwardly very different, occurred over a longer period, even to my 73rd birthday on December 9, 1998. Singularly meaningful events—synchronicities—came to me when they were most needed and can be described only as Helen Keller inferred, "They must be felt with the heart."

Dr. Carl G. Jung coined the word "synchronicity" after experiencing some deeply moving "unpredictable, unexplainable" coincidences which occurred throughout his psychiatric practice. Therefore, he defined a synchronicity simply as a meaningful coincidence without any apparent cause. I would add then that something is meaningful as it applied to the person to whom it is delivered, and having no apparent cause is the mystery only defined in the deeply personal recesses of one's own heart and soul. As Dr. Elizabeth Kubler Ross firmly stated in a lecture, "I believe there are no coincidences in life. I call them Divine Manipulations."

Even in the dark light of skeptical reality, history records thousands of "chance" and unrelated "incidents" which have proven to be the ramrods of human progress from astronomy to Zionology. You have only to read the reflections, notes, interviews, and biographies of highly esteemed world figures down through the ages to acknowledge this basic fact. For the plain and ordinary masses of us who have had such extraordinarily simple and beautiful signs touch our very souls, there is no further need to question or to doubt. Our very being is pierced by the truth and power of these personally meaningful happenings.

I am compelled to introduce my own helpful healing synchronicities with a most heart-rending story of a nurse friend of mine, Joan DiGiacomo. This happening about the death of her son is told in her own exact words:

Joseph was ten years old—almost eleven, as I'm sure he would want you to know—when he died from complications of Cystic Fibrosis in a Boston hospital. He was by all accounts a beautiful, brave, and perceptive child who endured numerous treatments and hospitalizations that seemed necessary in order to sustain his life.

On one April day, his physician, in a most kind and compassionate manner, informed my husband and me that we probably wouldn't be taking Joseph home from the hospital this time. And so, with feelings of utmost sadness, we approached Joseph's room. Although he had difficulty breathing and even talking, he still communicated with us through his beautiful "doe-like" soft brown eyes and hand gestures.

As it had been our custom, my husband and I took turns staying with him at night, as there was room for only one parent. On this particular night, it was my husband's turn to stay. As it came time for me to leave, I suspect Joseph sensed my uneasiness. As I gave him a hug and kiss before I left for the night, I saw him raise his frail hand in a "V" for victory, or for those familiar with the 60s and 70s, a peace sign. It seemed as though he was saying, "Don't worry, Mom. It's going to be all right." Not too many days later on a rainy Easter Saturday, Joseph succumbed to the long and devastating illness that robbed him of his life."

As my husband and I left the hospital, the sun came out and we then went to Cohasset, Massachusetts to spend the night with our relatives. The next morning was Easter Sunday and we attended church and then started the long, sad trip home to a town in upstate New York. As we were driving along an almost-deserted highway, I noted a car several feet ahead of us. As we came closer, I saw a little girl about nine or ten looking out the back window. As we came even closer, I noticed the little girl's hand was giving us a victory or peace sign. As I returned the sign to the child, I thought, "It's okay, Mom; everything is all right."

As you can plainly see, everything had to happen exactly on schedule for this event to take place: attend church at the right time, start home on an almost-deserted highway, meet a car with a little girl in the back seat. Then, from this little girl there was the "peace" sign, just what was needed (and cherished even now) for grieving parents in a state of shock and sorrow—"Divine Manipulations."

The Ladybug Connections

Now, I will relate the many and varied magical experiences that have occurred directly to me during these past years which absolutely leave me no doubt that they were sent from my heavenly love, Eileen. As you will notice, all of these experiences were a part of our daily lives, unceremoniously, before they were especially sent to me as a crutch in this now-lonely existence.

The first synchronicities came to me during the first summer after my girl's death, in the form of ladybugs, beautiful little creatures which had invaded Eileen's and my world.

Legend (from the Middle Ages) has it that ladybugs, or ladybird beetles, were thusly named in honor of the Virgin Mary. To most people, these little beetles are not repulsive as are many other insects. Ladybugs give the aura of fragility, beauty, and calmness, and seldom do they make us turn away or do we want to swat them. Their coloring is generally brilliant and uplifting.

The awareness and presence of ladybugs goes back in our family to when Mom and I were blessed with our first two children, our daughters Theresa and Nancy. They were only 16 months apart in age and were and continue to be a great joy to our family. As they grew from babies to little girls to young schoolchildren, my wife started to address them as "Ladybug." If they would ask a question or ask for something, or even require a loving word of discipline, she would punctuate her statements with, "Okay, Ladybug?" Or, "Do you understand, Ladybug?" My daughters still have a special feeling when they think of how she referred to them in this endearing fashion.

As time went on and our family grew from two little girls to three more boys and then our wonderful baby girl, we acquired a large, historic family abode. It had twelve-foot-high ceilings, five large bedrooms, two upstairs bathrooms, a large and livable attic, and, of course, a basement, which was my office. There were some years when the older girls occupied the privacy of the attic and when our #2 son Jimmy was in college, he made the rest of the basement his private quarters. We all remember the years at the big house with the greatest of happiness and pleasure. Our Eileen was the linchpin of the family. She had the most memorable gift of love, understanding, and common sense, and we all depended on her in every situation.

As our children grew to adulthood and started to begin their own adventures, this secure and wondrous home was too large for a now-shrinking family. Also, I was getting ready to retire from my private practice and continue my work with the county Health Department. It was at this fortuitous time that my sister-in-law Ann was making rounds with a real estate agent friend of hers. They came upon a 2½ acre area along the Wappingers Creek. It had a large main house and a small bungalow about 50 feet from the main house. There is a beautiful swimming pool behind the bungalow. It is a very pretty and private piece of property. Immediately, the thought came into Ann's head, "This is just the perfect home for Eileen and Joe," and also, creeping into her thoughts, "and the bungalow is just perfect for me." Well, to make a long story short: We saw it. We loved it. And as the timing was almost perfect, we bought it.

At this time, our two youngest, Nick and Eileen, were still living home. Eileen, our youngest, was presented, at last, with her own beautiful, large upstairs bedroom. It has a large picture window overlooking the swimming pool and the creek. Mom and I had the other large upstairs bedroom with a similar picture window and view. Nick had his own private bedroom downstairs. Now, I only tell you these seemingly unimportant details since the setting fits into some of my most exciting synchronicities. For as time went on, and only in Eileen's bedroom, in the corner of the picture window appeared ladybug after ladybug after ladybug. We couldn't find a nest, but they were all over the room, even sleeping with Eileen. This, to say the least, is quite unusual, as most species of ladybug and both adult and larval stages feed on insects harmful to plants, and ladybugs are helpful to farmers in destroying these insects.

Well, Mom and I spent a lot of time trying to rid Eileen's room of these really beautiful little beetles. Every so often we would close off Eileen's room and "bomb" it with special aerosols that were supposed to eliminate these ladybugs. Of course, Mom and I would have to close the rest of the house and go out for the day. Repeated attempts at this poisoning did not work, however, and Eileen ended up accepting the little creatures as roommates. From then on, ladybugs were a part of the special events in Mom's and my life.

One instance I recall very vividly involved an event when we were in New York City. Mom and I, with many other friends from PFLAG (Parents and Friends of Lesbians and Gays) joined the large June 1994 parade in support of these fine young men and women of our world. Mom was carrying one side of the Hudson Valley PFLAG banner, when all of the sudden in a pleasant and rather humorous voice she said, "Oh, look. There's a ladybug on our banner." And smiling, she said, "I think we will call it a gaydybug." Now how many times have any of you seen a ladybug in New York City? Fortunately, I can still hear my love's voice saying just this statement as she was recording her impressions of the parade on a tape recorder.

After my wife died, my life became unbearable, especially in the beginning. I have stated previously that I was living in a kind of semiconscious zombie state, hardly caring about anything in this world and often begging and pleading in an irrational mental condition just to die. I was still in this miserable state of mind during that first summer. I did everything I had to do out of duty and force of habit. It was during this first few months while I was working that I received unexpected gems of support from my loving and caring Eileen.

It was in July just a few months after my wife's death when I was driving alone in my car heading home from my hospital rounds. I remember the occasion exactly. The day was a sweltering, humid day. The windows had been closed in the car all day and the air conditioning was on full blast. As I was driving along, I began to think of my Eileen. My thoughts wandered. It really didn't matter anymore where I went or what I did. There was no one at home. My girl was gone! Suddenly, my whole being was overcome with the deepest, most penetrating grief and sorrow. I burst into an ocean of tears, crying like a baby. With tears flooding my face, I became insanely out of control. I started to scream, "I hate it! I hate it! I want to die!" I began to pound on the steering wheel, shaking from head to toe. I was emotionally in shock. I don't know how I made it back to my driveway, but I found myself sitting there in the car still crying uncontrollably.

All of a sudden, there it was! It struck me like lightning! There it was! Crawling out of the grill of the dashboard, there it was! A beautiful, quiet, calm ladybug appeared. How could that be? I just watched it walking on the dashboard. How could that be? Its presence seemed to take control of the situation. As I watched it, I began to calm down, to collect myself, to be in some sane control. I put my finger out to it and it crawled onto my finger and up to the back of my hand. Still somewhat dazed, I just watched it crawling around on the back of my hand. There it stayed and there I sat, for how long, I don't know. With my insanity and grief slowly subsiding, I regained my composure. I slowly relaxed and finally opened the car door. As the tension decreased and the tears dried, I got out of the car, and holding my hand outward, this special unexpected, beautiful little visitor just up and flew away, leaving me with the first magical moment of my lonely life. The love and new life of my dearest girl was being sent to me on the fragile wings of our life's connection.

But wait, you're not at all impressed with this ladybug story? Then let me tell you what happened to me just about one week later. Hey, you see ladybugs everywhere, all the time. Really? I don't think so. Well, I can only tell it to you like it happened. No frills, no jazz, the truth: just totally unexpected but completely enhancing a little joy for my gloomy and brittle heart.

This next experience again started as I was driving in my car, the same truly indescribably, wretched loneliness overwhelming my heart and soul. This time I was on my way to make rounds at the nursing home where I was medical director. The frustration of my life was again building up in me just as the last time. I was, of course, thinking of my Eileen and my unbelievable loss. I exploded in a rage of anger and self-pity. My wailing and sobbing knew no bounds. I pounded the seat and the steering wheel, again screaming, "I hate it! I hate it! I can't do it (live anymore). I can't take it. I hate it!" This outward, painful, lonely exhibition of my grief continued even as I pulled into the parking lot of the nursing home. I don't now know how I drove the car, how I managed to get there. Then I just sat there in the parking lot trying to contain my emotions, trying to stem the tears. Slowly my tears did subside and I regained some semblance of control of my emotions. I thought, "I can't make rounds in this condition. I must first go to the men's room and clear my head, prepare myself to be presentable during rounds."

I took a deep breath and headed directly and quickly to the men's room. This room is on the first floor off to one side and away from the busy part of the building. It is in the interior and has no windows and is not close to any doorway to the outside. As you enter, there is one main section which is common to most men's rooms. Toward the back is a private section which is entered through a partial metal door. As I usually do, I went to the back, closed the door, and turned toward the commode. My mind was instantly dazzled. It can't be! Do my eyes deceive me? No! Well, it really is...it's another ladybug. There it was just sitting at the corner on the wall about four feet up from the floor. There it was just sitting there. I was amazed and startled. Unbelievable! Totally unbelievable! Throughout my 24 years working at this nursing home, I had not seen one, not even one, ladybug. And, as a further fact, during my 20 years attending also at another nursing home, I had not seen one—not one—ladybug.

I really can't adequately describe my feelings. In an emotional sense, a weight, a weary, heavy weight, was lifted off my precarious nerves. I put my finger out to this beautiful little creature and again it just walked right into my hand. It walked around and around my hand, up the outside of my coat sleeve, and then it flew up to the ceiling by the light.

A joy, an inner peace and calmness, enveloped my consciousness, my whole being. My heart smiled and a little spark in my soul grew and energized me, carrying me through my rounds and throughout the day. My Eileen, my sweetest girl, was there watching over me, impressing deeply into my heart that I am not alone—no, not at all alone. As George Anderson said in *We Don't Die*, my wife, my total love, was just in "Outer Mongolia" and I would see her and be with her again. My faith was being renewed, reinvigorated, expanded. Carry on.

The Other Beetle

As I noted in the beginning of my account, many, many things happened during the first few years since my Eileen died to this world. I think the order and circumstances of these happenings were important in helping me to understand and believe that we are eternal beings. Therefore, other ladybug events have to await the proper time.

The other beetle, however, that intercepted my consciousness when I had climbed into bed hoping to fall right to sleep was what is referred to as a luminescent beetle, commonly called a firefly.

I have found the two most difficult times of the day for me to be just as I would awaken in the morning and when I retire at night and try to put the day behind me. This particular night was one of those agonizing, tossy-turny nights when my mind couldn't let go of the day and thoughts kept careening about my brain like a pinball bouncing around a pinball machine. The time of year was after my first summer alone, and my whole existence (my feelings, my life) was still in a state of anxiety, distress, and despair. However, with this continuous anxiety and sadness, I was beginning to grasp the truth of my faith about life after death. This night I was particularly questioning and vacillating over it. I was unable to get comfortable with my mind being tortured by thoughts of "there is a life after death; my girl is all right... but maybe not." "It is so. Maybe it isn't so," and on and on, and I'd get more and more irritated with myself. Finally, the real "me" broke in and said, "I believe." Then it said, "I believe 80%." Then, "No, no. I believe 90%." Then, "No. I believe 95%." Suddenly, with great resolve and indignation I barked at myself, "You dunce. You blockhead. You believe 100%. Your girl is all right. There is another life. You really do believe 100%. There is no doubt!" As I was debating with myself, I turned on my back.

I don't know why, but I opened my eyes in this dark room and my sight was focused on the corner of the window. It was a kind of sleepy focus, and I noticed what appeared to be a star sparkling far out in the sky. As my sight became clearer, I realized it's not a star. It's closer and it's flashing.

"It's a firefly!" As I watched it sparkling, flashing, it just sat there in the corner of the window. Not moving. Just flashing—period. About every five seconds there would be a flash of light. Startled, I sat up and wondered, "They just don't sit around. They dart here and there. They fly all over." I got out of bed and went to the window to inspect it more closely. As I got to the window, it flew away into the dark. Snap: just like that, it was gone. I thought, "It's late September. There shouldn't be any fireflies around, especially up here at the second floor." I looked out the window for some more flashing, for more fireflies. There was no flashing anywhere.

I must digress here and mention that when I first saw and realized there was a firefly flashing at my window and I was just lying there in bed, I began to experience the most exciting, tingly, ethereal sensation of my life. It was then that I repeated very strongly to myself, "Of course, you do believe 100%, and that firefly is specifically punctuating it for you."

Since I hadn't seen any more fireflies, I decided to go downstairs to the back deck and take a more careful look. As I reached the kitchen to go out to the back deck, my daughter-in-law, Jean, came downstairs. She had heard me and worried if I was feeling all right. I told her my whole story and together we went out to the deck to search for fireflies. We didn't find one, not one firefly. Now, believe what you will, I saw one, and the timing of that little beetle's appearance was just perfect. Yes, that one luminescent bug was there for a reason. To Jean, a computer expert, and to me, a scientifically oriented physician, the reason was startlingly obvious. My faith and belief were again being reinforced by an event (synchronicity) from just one little flashing beetle. "Of course! I believe 100%." And my faith has never wavered or diminished since that pure, intense, and particular moment. My loneliness and grief has at times been almost overpowering and disheartening. But my faith has remained constant and strong.

Birds, Birds, and More Birds

As I have mentioned previously, the last nine-plus years with my wife were spent at our "retirement" home along the Wappingers Creek in Dutchess County. Those two acres of land along the creek gave us some of the most private, peaceful, and beautiful times of our lives. We saw all kinds of birds, animals, and fish in and around the creek. We were inundated with Canadian geese, whose unmistakable jabbering at 4 a.m. announced that soon another day would be dawning. We watched them fly with grace and beauty as they would take off and land on the creek. Sometimes there were so many of them swooping in for a landing that we were sure they would crash into each other. It never happened!

There were so many large, black crows that one day when they all lifted off from the same tree, hundreds of them, they completely blocked out the sun as they rose to fly across the creek to their feeding grounds. It was very eerie and impressive.

Once in a while we would see a stately heron standing at the water's edge on its long, reed-like legs, a fragile beauty giving the impression of strength and majesty. Then there were the colorless wild turkeys, those ugly muscular birds that can hardly fly. Are they really the ancestors of the "butterball?" Only once did they venture up to our backyard, just a few feet from our living room picture window. We were so excited watching them strut. There were six of them. My wife and I got our camera to take their picture. We laughed and talked about those six turkeys and showed off their pictures often.

There were the diminutive, dainty hummingbirds, darting and dashing here and there, aimlessly it seemed. There were doves and many other birds that I didn't recognize. We put up bird feeders and Mom or I would brave the cold, the snow, and ice to see that these fragile, lovely creatures had enough food during the winter months.

My beautiful Eileen was a true nature-lover, gentle and caring of all God's creatures...

AND...

She didn't forget to contact me through her affection for them and her love for me.

A view of the creek

The Turkey Connection

It was the morning of November 13 the year after Mom died, and I was home preparing for the day's work. As County Medical Examiner, I was on-call most of the time, day or night. This day, I was called by the police to investigate a drowning at the outskirts of the City of Poughkeepsie. I live about half-an-hour from the city, and usually take the Salt Point turnpike as the most direct way from my house to the city. I can't leave the front door of my home without saying a prayer for my Eileen and telling her I love her. Also, as I have indicated, I do a lot of driving and spend a lot of time alone thinking about her and talking to her.

This day as I drove out of the neighborhood and onto the turnpike, I started to talk to my girl as usual. Generally, I talk about memories and things we did together, or I commune about what I should or should not do about one thing or another. Our minds were mostly on the same track, so it really does help. I go on and on like a broken record. This day, however, it hit me that I was jabbering and jabbering and I just stopped. It occurred to me that I was b-o-r-i-n-g.

Then I said, "Mom, I know you must have better things to do than listen to me jabber. There have to be wonderful things for you to do 'up there.' Don't pay attention to me. You don't have to listen to me. You are probably far away, so don't bother about me. I'm just a pain! You can't be around here listening to me all the time."

Meanwhile, I arrived at the scene of the drowning. It was about noontime and I investigated the conditions and circumstances of this tragedy with the police. After I examined the body, I made arrangements for it to be brought to St. Francis Hospital for an autopsy. Time was getting on in the afternoon when I started back home on the turnpike. The Salt Point Turnpike is a fairly well traveled county road with many curves and a few good straightaways. I was about half way home along a straightaway when I noticed there was something in my lane about a quarter of a mile ahead. As I came closer, it looked like there were a few birds standing in the road. I began to slow down a little and watched for other cars. There were no cars coming in either direction. When I was about 100 feet from the birds, I realized there were two "wild turkeys" standing in my lane. I slowed even more and actually had to stop about 25 feet from them. There were no other cars on the road. The turkeys really paid no attention to me and finally, taking their sweet time, they started to walk across the road. Then, they went airborne, sort of, in their awkward, lumbering way, and flew into the field. There still were no cars coming in either direction. I started on my way, picking up speed, when it hit me. Hey, Mom is around lots of times, and she hears me. Of course! No doubt! Why would two usually evasive wild turkeys definitely stop me? Why? Why would two mostly unsocial turkeys stand unconcerned in the road with this monster car bearing down on them? How many times has this happened to anyone driving on this road? I haven't heard of such a thing. It seemed like they knew I would stop, wouldn't hurt them, would give them the right of way. A coincidence? Of course! A synchronicity? Exactly. A meaningful answer to my questions and statements to my wonderful wife Eileen.

There are starting to add up, these "coincidences." And there are many more of them, all from my Eileen, giving me the wisdom, courage, faith, and stamina to go on here— without her.

I will always love *wild turkeys!*

Wild turkeys in the yard

March 20, 1997

At the beginning of this chapter, I said that it was one of the most important and significant chapters of this book. Now, however, I will write one of the most significant events of this chapter, as well as one of the most endearing events of my life. I think of this HAPPENING often, and especially when I am in a very dejected, lonely frame of mind.

Many of us, unfortunately, have a closed outlook on the most precious gifts of our lives. We may stubbornly refuse to accept and generally can't even conceive of the many paranormal treasures that the world and our God offer to us for the support of our bodies and our souls. I would be truly surprised—even astonished—if anyone would not be moved to at least consider this next event in my life which occurred on March 20, 1997, the first anniversary of my beloved Eileen's death.

I must digress and describe certain peculiar "white things," we called them (see photo), that were ever-present outside our upstairs bedroom picture window. And were these unknown little creatures given to us for the specific occasion of the first anniversary of my Eileen's journey into our eternal world? During the nine years we lived in our "retirement" home, these little "white things" clung to the outside of the screen of our upstairs picture window.

Sometimes there were as many as 40 or 50 of them, and they never seemed to move. To Eileen and me, the uninitiated to the world of insects, they appeared to be very fragile and mysterious. They were a topic of conversation and conjecture for us. We really didn't notice them anywhere else around the house. And so it went from year to year—they were always present.

I didn't know anything about them when my Eileen died. However, the absolutely marvelous synchronicity which occurred on March 20, 1997 tweaked my curiosity and finally solidified my resolve to find out about them.

It was in late June of 1996, the summer after my wife had died, that I moved into the little cottage about 50 feet from our big house, which I gave to Theresa, our oldest daughter, and her family. There were no "white things" anywhere on the screens of the little cottage. I lived there all the rest of 1996 and into April of 1997, when I moved in with my son Jimmy and his family at the discretion and insistence of my six "kids." (I guess he got the short straw!) It was in early April that the addition to his house would be ready for me.

While I was living in the cottage, March 20, 1997 came along, the first anniversary of my beautiful Eileen's departure from this world. My children and I planned to attend Mass together in memory of our special wife and mother. I remember this March 20 very, very well, almost exactly. I can still see myself as I arose from bed and shuffled into the bathroom on this bright and sunny day. The bathroom of the cottage faces the roadway, which is just the opposite side of the property from where the creek flows. As I sleepily looked out of the bathroom window, I was startled, aroused, totally amazed, and, I would have to admit, visibly shaken and somewhat dumbfounded. There on the outside window screen was one—exactly one—exquisite, fragile "white thing." My heart began to pound. My mind began to race. It can't be! It took quite a few seconds for me to regain my composure, to realize and understand the overwhelming beauty and significance of this wonderful event, the appearance of one little "white thing" on March 20, 1997. My whole being became engrossed in this inspirational message that my one and only beloved was sending me. You see, this event was very clear and intimate and very connected between us. The anxiety and sadness of this occasion was partly removed from my heavy heart.

Together, in our prayers, and later at lunch, the mood of all of us took on a more lighthearted and joyful aura. Our precious gift, our loving Mom, really, truly had not died, but was watching over us and sharing this day with us, and telling us so in a way that we could comprehend and assimilate into our very souls.

Now, hold on, before you prematurely pass judgment on this exciting After-Death Communication (ADC). Let me give you the core element of this synchronicity, this very, very meaningful coincidence. The crux of the matter is as follows.

My sister-in-law Ann lived in this very cottage all the years while my Eileen and I occupied the big house. During those nine years, she never once saw a "white thing" at this cottage—anywhere. And, as I have stated previously, the summer after my Eileen died and through that winter up to the day of March 20, 1997, I did not see one—not even one—of those mysterious little creatures while I lived in the cottage. Finally, on September 18, 1998, those little "white things" were identified for me by the Cornell Cooperative

Extension program in Millbrook, New York. They are the mayfly subimago exoskeletons, the winged flying stage of which precedes the final molt to becoming an adult, when they release themselves from their skeletons in preparation for mating.

Just one little "white thing" inexplicably found its way to where none of its cousins had ever landed, and to my heart, on March 20, 1997, exactly one year to the day that my love left this world and started on her own special journey to paradise, the wonder which we will never fully grasp until we, each and every one of us, cross the barrier of our own death. As one of my friends said to me when I told him, "I can hardly wait to be with her," — "It will happen."

Mayfly ("white things") on the window screen

More Ladybugs

It was only about six weeks after the wonderful appearance of the "white things," mayfly, that another ladybug coincidence entered our family lives in May of 1997. During the first week of May, my son, Jimmy, decided to take his family to Mom's and my timeshare. He took the family for a long weekend and was somewhat amazed by another ladybug connection.

A two-hour drive from where we live in Dutchess County takes us to Shawnee-on-the-Delaware, Pennsylvania, a beautiful spot set just off the Delaware Water Gap in the foothills of the Pocono Mountains. Mom and I had the most relaxed and unforgettable days together at that peaceful resort area. We would awaken at our leisure in the morning and together prepare the most delicious breakfast to begin our day of joy and fun. Some days we would just stay at our rustic cabin and spend the afternoon reading and relaxing before taking off to one of the little intimate restaurants in the area. Some of our best days, however, were spent wandering and walking hand-in-hand along the quiet virgin woods of the Pocono foothills, just reveling in God's gift of beauty in nature. We looked forward with much anticipation to our vacations at Shawnee and spent many blissful days in communion with our souls as our love grew deeper and stronger in God's presence.

Everyone in our family enjoyed vacations at Shawnee. When Jimmy unlocked the cabin door and entered the cabin, he found a flyer entitled, "Ladybug, ladybug, fly away...please!" At first, he smiled at the references to our well-known little creatures and went ahead unloading his car and preparing for a pleasant respite with his family. Later, as he looked over the curious flyer, he noticed the date, March 20, 1996, the exact date of Mom's death. This little circular had survived a year and six weeks just to tell Jimmy, "all the ladybug incidents in your family are real, very real, and I stayed here in this cabin just to emphasize the downright truth of these wonderful, oft-occurring synchronicities. I survived the cleaning lady, the cabin repairman, the innumerable other guests, for a year and six weeks to stamp my approval on the wisdom of this one elegant fact. Mom is alive and well, smiling down on all of you."

Just another coincidence!

I have had after-death communications during these past three years, more wonderful than I could have envisioned, which continued to enhance in my heart the faith and belief that we don't die, that we are truly eternal beings created and loved by the Architect of the Universe. I will continue with these explicit experiences in future chapters.

But now, here are more wonderful gifts from my girl, our God, and our unusual ladybug connection.

It was a little over a year after my Eileen died that I moved into my comfortable in-house apartment with Jimmy, Jean, and my grandchildren.

During this change in my life, I developed a routine, or as much of a routine as possible for a physician/medical examiner. I would make hospital rounds, do office work, and return home between 3:30 and 4:00 p.m. Of course, there were times when my day began at 4:00 a.m. and stretched out to late in the day, so it all evened out in the long run.

Usually, I have office mail, newspapers, books, journals, a drink of soda or juice, and other odds and ends with me when I get home in the afternoon. I also pick up the mail at the end of our long driveway. It sometimes takes two or three trips up the driveway before I get everything into the house. Also, one day a week, the garbage cans have been emptied and are at the roadway at the edge of the driveway. I usually take them back to the house. Why am I telling you all of this? Read on!

This particular day in May, as I was driving home, I

was as always talking to my Eileen. I remember very well as I drove up the neighborhood road and turned into our driveway what I was saying to her: "I love you, Mom, and I just miss you so much. You are the best, in every way the best, the best wife, the best mother, and the best person in the world to me. I just love you so much." And as I stopped and opened the car door, I asked her, "But where are you, Mom? Are you right here sort of parallel to us or are you far away?" When I was out of the car, I noticed it was garbage can day. I had a lot of "stuff" with me and also wanted to get the home mail, so it took me a few trips. After the second trip, I said to myself that I ought to get the garbage cans and not leave them for Jimmy. So I traipsed back to the street to get them. We have three large plastic garbage cans and two have attached covers. The other one has a separate cover, usually lying somewhere along the edge of the road. It takes me two trips to return the three cans. I bent down to pick up the loose cover and was just about to cover the can when—whoops!—walking sprightly around the edge of the can was, you guessed it, a beautiful, gentle, little ladybug. Wow! I was totally surprised and excited. I had just asked "my sweetest girl" where she was, and there in plain sight was our special connection. It clearly was indicating to me that she is with me and sees and hears me, more than I can envision. Mom was telling me, "My spirit is watching over you, and with you very often. I love you." That's what she was saying to me through our lovely little beetle. I know, because that is the kind of care and closeness we always had for each other.

Was this another synchronicity? My faith and wisdom leave me no doubt. But for any unbelievers, as they say in the West, "Listen up." That wonderful day in May was the first day I had seen a ladybug around our house. All summer of the previous year I had not seen one ladybug. Again, I say I did not see even one of those wonderful little beetles. I ask you, was that little creature a loner? The Lone Ranger? Maybe it had been banished from its community to live alone?

It is now the end of the year, 1998, as I write. I have yet to see another ladybug here. Did you know that ladybugs don't travel alone? Did you know that they always stick together in nests? There are always a slew of them around if you take the time to look. Well, I took the time to look for them all of 1998 and I saw only one. All of 1998, I saw only one ladybug around our property, and it came to me in answer to my question, "But where are you, Mom?" God works in strange and wonderful ways—Divine Manipulations.

Oh, by the way, I put my finger out to it and it climbed right on and walked around on my hand as I took the garbage can to the back of the house. Then, it flew away. It just up and flew away. Thank you, my sweetest girl.

December 9, 1998

It has been almost three years since my beautiful Eileen died to this world, March 20, 1996. Every day since then has been totally horrible for me. I know I'll be with her again, and I look forward to that time with a compelling anticipation. However, deep inside me, there is an unquenchable fire of loneliness and loss which at times rages so vehemently as to almost consume my very soul. My anger explodes so suddenly and so violently that I wonder why my God doesn't destroy me for my ungraciousness toward Him. I do know that His love and mercy sustains me during these explosive times and also during the times of quiet resignation. I carry on with great difficulty, but fully aware of His unconditional love for all of us, which we humanly fail to recognize or completely understand. The closest I can come to understand this total and unconditional love is through the truly brilliant love that is shared by my

Eileen and me. Although I have reflected before that generally my days are horrible (humanly, without her, there is no attainable joy), my intuition, knowledge, and understanding of His mercy generally keeps me on an even keel in these especially rough waters. As St. Peter stated, "We have an inheritance of inexpressible joy."

It was thus on December 9, 1998 when I was floating along rather calmly that I expressed to my beautiful Eileen, "Today is my birthday, my love. Can you send me a present?" I was teasing her, of course, and inwardly seeing and enjoying her precious, radiant smile. Well, as the day wore on, I started home from my rounds. (When you are 73, who needs a birthday, or for that matter, a birthday present?)

It was late afternoon when I turned off a side road onto the Salt Point Turnpike. I had only gone 100 or so yards on the turnpike when I was forced to stop. No, there wasn't an accident. In fact, there were no cars coming in either direction. However, now really envision this. There were at least 300 or 400 birds just sitting in the roadway. Also, there were "a bunch more" in the trees on each side of the road. They didn't seem to be startled or anxious. They just sat there on the road chirping away. They just sat there for what seemed the longest time, maybe 30 or 40 seconds. They did not move off the road. (Sit in your car in the middle of a busy road for just half a minute and observe how long it really is.) Finally, a group of them, 20 or 30, took off and flew into the field. Every five or ten seconds, another group of them would take off and fly into the field. This scenario was repeated until the road was clear. Mind you, during this whole episode, there were no other cars coming along. None.

I started up again and as I slowly drove along the turnpike, it began to dawn on me. It hit me! This time it hit me right in the head! No way this could just happen! No Way!

Impossible! Suddenly, a blissful smile crossed my face and I said, "Thanks for the present, Mom. I love you."

Surely this was just another coincidence. We always see hundreds of birds just sitting on a busy roadway with no concern for a car bearing down on them. Just another coincidence. Not to me it wasn't! My sweetest girl sent me a special present, the best birthday present I ever had, one I will never forget.

Another Ladybug "Coincidence"

True scientists believe there are no coincidences. That's how questions are formed into theories. The more consistent happenings that occur, the better credence is given to a theory. In like manner, when something happens once, there are no odds. However, if an unusual happening keeps reoccurring, the odds against it just being "mere coincidence" get higher and higher.

This will be the fourth ladybug occurrence of an unusual nature that I will describe. None of these are "mere" coincidences. They all happened under very special circumstances that directly stamped a purpose on each incident.

That is not even including the incidents of the mayfly and the firefly. You judge for yourself.

My six-year-old grandson was given a birthday party at Discovery Zone. All the young relatives went to the party. However, my daughter Nancy and I stayed home to care for six-month-old Christopher who was deemed too young for the party. The party was on March 27, 1999. It lasted all afternoon and everyone returned home around 5:30 p.m. Well, after all our hard work caring for Chris, Nancy and I decided to go out for dinner. We went to Copperfield's, a well-known restaurant not far from home. When we arrived, the parking lot looked quite full, however, we went in and were taken to a quiet side room. This room has booths along the side walls which comfortably fit four people. Each booth has a chandelier hanging down over the middle of each table to about 2 ½ feet above the table.

Nancy and I settled in and were each given a menu. We ordered drinks while we reviewed the menu. The waitress brought cocktails, but we were not ready to order. As I was reviewing the menu, something dropped from the chandelier onto my placemat, but I paid it no attention. Nancy, however, smiling, said, "Look, Dad." I looked down at the placemat, and there in front of me was a beautiful little ladybug. What do you think of that? Well, need I tell you what we thought?

Beautiful. Just beautiful! Figure the odds of that just happening. This little creature stayed with us all through our meal. It just continued to walk around the table totally without fear. As we were ready to leave the restaurant, it walked to one side of the table against the wall and disappeared down the side. Ladybugs can fly. They don't just fall straight down like lumps of mud.

When I paid the check, I asked the cashier if they had ladybugs around the restaurant. She looked quite surprised and mumbled something to the effect of, "Well, maybe on occasion." If so, this was the perfect occasion for our Eileen to tell Nancy and me, "Hello" and "Enjoy your meal."

Just another ladybug coincidence, not really of any consequence. By the way, how many ladybugs have jumped down on your dinner table and stayed for an hour?

It is very clear to me that our ladybug connection is firm, stable, and eternal, as is our love. Again, thank you, my love, and thank you, my God!

CHAPTER
FIVE

WORDS AND MUSIC

"Music is love in search of a word."

—*Sidney Lanier*

My beautiful Eileen and I are both music lovers. Eileen was more open to all types of music than I, and she had a place in her heart for the great classics to the modern rock and roll. I prefer classical and the Big Band music of the 30s, 40s, and 50s, since I played saxophone in swing bands in high school and college. We loved listening to music and had records from the 78 rpms and V-discs of World War II, to our present CDs. We also had piano sheet music that dated back as far as the 30s, since Eileen took piano lessons during her early school years.

Among all the synchronicities I had experienced, the most rapturous were those happenings involving music of our younger days which impressed my conscious and subconscious moments—the kind of music I played in our swing bands. My love sent me not only the music, but the words fit perfectly into my heart. I know they came from my Eileen.

Three episodes occurred over the past six years that filled my heart with reassurance and carried me through some very difficult and lonely moments. I play these special songs in my head and in my heart when the need for them is especially crucial, and tears of sadness and joy touch my cheeks.

Specifically, the second and third After Death Communications impress on my mind my dear wife's continued presence and the truth of our eternal love for each other.

However, the first synchronicity happened while I was fully awake and driving somewhere. I don't remember exactly where. Actually, since my Eileen died, I can't bring myself to listen to music very often. In fact, I never play our records or CDs when I'm at home because the memories tear me apart.

When I am driving my car, I listen to sports and news broadcasts about 95% of the time. Once in a great while, when the news and sports broadcasts are continually repeated, I may switch to a music station of my liking, or just snap the radio off altogether.

This "special" day I was driving along with the radio blaring away, and I was also talking to my girl. I was telling her again how great it was when she was here with me, and I said, "You are my earthly angel." The radio was a total bore and I decided to change to a music station. As I turned to the station, someone was singing these exact words of a song from my Big Band days. "You are my special angel, sent from above." (*My Special Angel*, words and music by Jimmy Duncan). The words and the tune I know very well, but I bet that many of you under age 40 have never heard this song. In point of fact, I have not heard it being played or sung anywhere since my band-playing days. I was so excited and overjoyed because (1) I very seldom—practically never—refer to Eileen as my angel. I mostly call her my sweetest girl or my Eileen; (2) the timing of the words and the music was perfect—to a "T"—to the second when I was calling Eileen my "earthly angel."

Well, it was just another incidental chance occurrence, really of no consequence. Maybe so, but not to me! This song gave me the help and perseverance to get through another day. The curious thing about this chance occurrence is that this song became very popular for a short while after the war years and then faded away to be replaced by the music of the changing styles of the Beatles and Elvis. The whole scope of popular music took a radical change from then on.

Now, what's even more curious is this: About a week later, give or take a day, I was in the same exact scenario. I was wide awake, driving somewhere, with the radio blaring. The news and the sportscasts were being repeated as they generally are when these stations run out of anything else "wonderful or horrible" to recount, and I haphazardly tuned to a station with music. Hallelujah! Don't tell me! But, wow, and yes, yes, yes! That exact instant—those exact words, "You are my special angel, sent from above," coming through to me, the timing exquisite and perfect to a "T," to the very second that I turned to the channel, a beautiful, melodious synchronicity. In my heart my beautiful Eileen was saying, "Hi, Dad. I love you." Of course, just balderdash. Same old coincidence. Hey, not to me! To me it was one of Elizabeth Kubler-Ross's "Divine Manipulations."

Of course, there couldn't possibly be more of such shenanigans...or...well, read on!

I remember the exact times of the other two synchronicities involving music sent directly to my heart, straight as an arrow, but definitely intimating the paranormal.

I was visiting my son Nick and his family in Palo Alto, California. It was on the first Sunday of Advent when Nick and I were attending Mass in San Francisco with our special friend Sean-Patrick. During the Mass it was announced that in the afternoon the church choir and musicians would be putting on a program of Christmas music. Sean-Patrick told us that this particular program was exceptional and very inspiring. We decided to have lunch, catch up on our lives, and then return to enjoy the program. We did just that and enjoyed an afternoon of Christmas songs and hymns. Nick and I then headed back to Palo Alto after a warm good-bye to Sean-Patrick.

All during this pleasant day and on the way home, in the quiet recesses of my heart and mind there was a constant loneliness and anxiety for my wonderful Eileen. You see, this is exactly the kind of day my Eileen would have relished.

As I remember it, the evening was quiet and uneventful, but I was still "wiped out" with an inner turmoil, missing her so very much. I went to bed and finally to sleep with a heavy heart. I awoke about 3:30 a.m., I judged, as it was still dark outside. Nothing outwardly had disturbed me and I remember saying to myself, "It's still dark, not time to get up yet," and I just turned over and tried to get comfortable. At this very moment a song impressed itself beautifully and peacefully into my sleepy consciousness. I know the tune and the words very well. As it played in my mind, my heart started singing the words. "Because of you there's a song in my heart, because of you, my romance had its start." (*Because of You,* words and music by Arthur Hammerstein and Dudley Wilkinson) On and on the tune and words filled my soul as I fell back to sleep.

When I awoke and realized what had occurred during those wakeful moments (this was definitely not a dream), I knew—no doubt—none—that my Eileen had been reminding me of our perfect and beautiful life on this earth. I can still see myself turning over in bed to get into a relaxed position. (The tears are flowing now as I sing those words to her and as I recount this very incident while I am alone in my room.)

What is very exciting and even more special to me about this synchronicity was that, of course, I wasn't thinking of this song or any song, for that matter. My mind was on a straight track to go back to sleep. Also, although this is well known to Eileen and me, it is not special to our hearts and romance. It's just a popular song that we both know well. However, the words told me perfectly that she loves me and that we are still one and together. Again, the timing of this event gave me the unequivocal awareness of her presence and eternal love. This wonderful happening without any provocative thought on my part requires no explanation and no questioning. It is the power of love, which transcends every barrier. It is another gift from my wife, through our Creator, to a lonely man whose life is in disarray and utter turmoil. It is one more way that my Eileen has found to tell me that we will be together again.

I can tell you quite frankly that songs don't just pop into my head during my sleep or during my waking hours. It just doesn't happen. My wife and I used to fall asleep listening to music (and holding hands—we always held hands), but I can't bring myself to listen to music much any more.

I did, however, have another wonderful song touch my heart, and I won't ever forget the date because what happened early that morning left me in such a state, so excited and joyful, that you will see, it is difficult to describe in mere words. This is exactly what happened during the early morning of January 19, 1999, when I was not really awake and not fully asleep. People who study sleep patterns would probably call it an hypnogogic state—somewhere between complete awareness and deep slumber.

I was comfortable and warm; kind of feeling it was getting light outside without really looking. Not, "Hey, I'm awake...it's too early." More like floating on a bed of puffy clouds. Now, while my mind was contemplating whether it was awake or asleep, a song edged its way into my semiconsciousness. It was a gentle and soft melody flowing through my head. And the words, the words were nectar to my spirit: "Sweetheart, if you should stray a million miles away, I'll always be in love with you." (*I'll Always Be in Love with You* by Bud Green, Herman Ruby and Sam H. Stept). I grasped the words and held them tightly in my heart. Where did they come from? That's an old love song, not one that I carried around in my "bag of tricks" just waiting to burst through. I have never thought of this song; I don't remember even hearing it since I once played it at a dance some 50 years ago. There it was, soothing my soul, filling my cup with love. Say what you will. Explain it away with a laugh and a smile. Our worlds, Eileen's and mine, do touch each other through the graciousness of God's compassion and mercy.

Now, that song does pop into my head regularly, reminding me that "a million miles away" is just a turn of the knob when it is my time to go through that unknown door. My sweetest girl, I can hardly wait to join you in that paradise of joy and love. Again, as George Anderson states, "It is only like being in Outer Mongolia and I can't see you for a while."

CHAPTER
SIX

A CALL FROM HEAVEN

In Aramaic, "Death" translates to
"Not Here; Present Elsewhere."

I have been thinking about how to write this chapter for months. In fact, I have started a couple of times and the writing didn't fit into my head and my heart the way I felt it and still see it everyday in my thoughts.

So, here goes again! What is so difficult about it is what happened on that mysterious Saturday afternoon in August of 1997 is so unbelievably exciting, so unbelievably beautiful, so unbelievable but true, and so spiritually wonderful to me. I never in my wildest hopes had considered this would happen to me. Yes, in my reading and research I had come across this ADC phenomenon, but I never ever considered, never even gave one thought of it happening to me. It reaffirms everything I have written and felt to the depth of my own very lonely soul; that there is no death. We are eternal and our love transcends every obstacle, every dimension.

Well, what happened? What keeps me floating on a cloud

when I need it most? I would really like to start from the beginning of this episode because the pieces fit together so beautifully, and let it unwind as it did that August.

My son, Joe, has a good friend who is a real estate agent. While Joe was talking with him one day, the idea unfolded that Joe might be able to rent a house on the New Jersey shore for a week during the height of the summer season. It now had been a little over a year since Mom died to this world and there was still a tremendous amount of shock and grief involved in our everyday affairs. Joe got together with his brothers and sisters and they decided to pick a week in August when they all would plan to be free to vacation together at the Jersey shore. Everyone—brothers and sisters, spouses and children—would spend a week together in joyous camaraderie of love and fun. Nick, his wife Christine and children even came in from California for this vacation. There were 22 of us, and in fact we had to rent two houses to fit all of us. Well, the plan worked magnificently and it was a wonderful week of fun, playing, teasing repartee together. Sometimes we ate out and sometimes "volunteers" would make "exquisite" breakfast or supper.

The care and love we showered on each other made it one of the most memorable weeks of my life. The one glitch for all of us—and especially me, although we didn't dwell on it, was that one predominant piece of the puzzle was missing. Although I tried not to reveal it, I carried a very heavy heart every waking hour.

One incident was especially difficult for me and I think of it once in a while with my baggage of sadness. It was decided that we should have a picture of all of us to remember this special occasion. Christine managed the photography as we all draped ourselves in one way or another in and around the sofa. She set the timer on the camera and rushed in to join us for this "epic" photograph. Everything went on schedule perfectly. The one thing that kept tugging at my heart, of course; my sweet and wonderful Eileen wasn't going to be in the picture. I secretly entertained the idea, one that I had read about, that she would in some way impress herself into the picture for this momentous occasion. In some unknown fashion, we would see her when the photo was developed. Well, to be sure, this did not happen—but, here is the family as recorded in August 1997, a tribute to my beautiful Eileen.

The Ross Family,
Long Beach Island, New Jersey, Summer 1998

Top Row, left to right: Jimmy Ross Jr.; Patrick Herrmann; Jim Osborn; Jim Ross; Jean Ross; Christine Evans; Nick Ross; Marie Osborn; Eileen Osborn

Middle Row, left to right: Joseph Ross III; Kelsey Herrmann; Joseph Ross IV; Nancy Ross; Joseph Ross Jr.; Theresa Osborn; Nancy Ann Osborn; Eileen Ross

Bottom Row, left to right: Mary Beth Ross; Jimmy Osborn Jr.; Katelyn Lehman; Carli Ross; Brad Lehman

As I have indicated, that week's vacation with all of us together was very special and wonderful. On the final Saturday morning we all gathered into our individual cars and started back to our homes. Jimmy and his family and I arrived home Saturday afternoon. I went upstairs and lay across my bed to divest my heart of its infinite depth of sadness and loneliness.

I have to now digress and describe what was a pointed "coincidence" to this whole drama, which for me, ended with sheer ecstasy. The day before we started our vacation, Nick had to go to the Poughkeepsie railroad station; I forget exactly why. A fender-bender occurred with my car and the car of a friend while he was there. I called my friend and told him to do whatever was necessary and we would work it out when I returned from vacation. With that settled, we went on our vacation.

Now, that Saturday afternoon when we returned from vacation, and while I was lying on my bed, I remembered the fender-bender. Therefore, while I was thinking about it, I called my friend. He was not at home, and I left a message for him on his answering machine. It was not five minutes later when the telephone rang and I thought, "That must be my friend." I rolled over in bed and picked the receiver up to my ear. As I was about to say, "Hello," I heard the most unusual sounds coming from the telephone. I must try to describe them as completely and carefully as I can. The sounds were of the ocean waves and the tide as they rushed to the shore—just as we heard during the dead of night on our vacation—just as we all have experienced when we put a large seashell to our ear. Along with those well-recognized sounds of the roar of the waves, and in the background there was the static and crackling that we have all heard, like a ham radio transmission, or a ship's radio calling for help when in a storm at sea. Before I had the chance to try and interpret what was happening, I heard a low voice coming through the receiver—a voice I didn't recognize—and I clearly heard the following message: "J-o-o-o-o-o-o-o-e . . . my sweetheart—!"

I repeat, I clearly heard those words above all the background sounds on the telephone. That was all the voice said. I waited and listened and waited, only to hear the continuous roaring of the waves and static-like radio-cackle. Finally, I put the receiver down.

It is impossible to fully describe my state of mind during those wonderful minutes. It suddenly exploded in my head and heart. Eileen—only my Eileen would say that to me. My body was tingling—I don't know how to actually describe it as all these things were happening. During this excitement I was trying to digest and interpret the voice and those eerie sounds. My brain was trying to recapture every second of that experience while trying to arrange it into some semblance of human order and understanding. I was amazed and befuddled.

However, within those few minutes the telephone rang again, before I could fully review and think about this wonderful experience. I answered the telephone in a sort of dazed mood and was abruptly awakened. It was my friend returning my call. We discussed the details of the minor accident and I returned the receiver to its holder.

Now, I really delved into every aspect of my "telephone call from heaven."

1. Yes, it was real—very real—not a sham. My Eileen would surely contact me after such a wonderful, lonely, horrible, week. As she had many other times, she would carry me over the hump of my hard times. I established in my intellect and common sense; in my wisdom, faith and integrity; yes it was my beautiful, "radiant" Eileen calling out to me.

2. The telephone was in perfect working condition. Eileen's call had come between two routine and normal

calls. They all occurred within a total time-span of 15 to 20 minutes.

3. That Saturday afternoon in August 1997 was a typical, hot and clear summer's day. The whole eastern seaboard was in calm weather. There were no storms, no lightning, no unsettled weather.

4. I was awake, of sound mind and body, making rational decisions and judgments when this happened.

5. Here are references from other accounts of telephone calls: *Visitation from the Afterlife. True Stories of Love and Healing* by Lee Lawson, page 47: *Hill Country* by Michael Drummond Davidson, and *Hello From Heaven* by Bill and Judy Guggenheim, Chapter 12, page 161: Person-to-Person Telephone ADCs

However, what is of major importance in our human existence to understand, as a great many of us do, is the Truth that "God is Love." The love of our Creator is perfect and unconditional. We in our human nature know this through our own consciousness, and we all practice this love to some degree during our lives. Some of us, of course, are so egocentric that we reject even the basics of human love for the more enticing frailties like greed, power, and self-gratification.

However, many of us who have had the good fortune to experience true human love in it's near perfect Godlike proportions, know that this gift tops all—tops everything else in this universe.

This total love of my Eileen and me is, I believe, unexcelled in this world. The energy of this Divine love can overcome all other energies be they electric, nuclear, or the energy of hate.

Whoever said, "Love conquers all," knew exactly what she/he was saying.

Thank you my true and only Love.

CHAPTER
SEVEN

THERE ARE SUCH THINGS

"Men may be mortal, but MAN is immortal."
— *New York Daily News cartoon, 10/20/99*

The world is continually bombarded with <u>literally</u> <u>thousands</u> of unpredictable, <u>unexplainable</u>, and truly exciting spiritual happenings. This chapter involves a flurry of very intriguing phenomena, which I hope will give you pleasure and invite your curiosity to explore our amazing world with an open mind and loving heart.

I'd like to begin with something that happened one night when I was awakened by a telephone call from the head nurse at the local hospital. I can't explain this surprising happening, but I know in my heart that it was another gift from "my sweetest girl."

Let me set the stage for you, because I am amazed every day when I review what happened and I say to my girl, "How'd you do that, my girl?"

Eileen and I have a very sturdy bed which I still use. It is one of those hardwood heavy beds with drawers along each of the sides. The front headboard is really a bookcase attached and immovable from the bed. The top shelf of this bookcase has a number of things on it, including a lamp that my wife painted for me, plus some pottery figures and a special book of poems which my wife used to read before she went to sleep.

This night I went to sleep about 11:00 p.m., which is around my usual time to turn in. At about 2:00 a.m. I was awakened by a telephone call from my answering service. The operator said that she had been paging me. I was surprised at that because during the night the service phones me instead of paging me. I said, "You usually telephone me. Why did you page me?" Then I said, "Okay, what is it?" At that moment I heard the pager go off, but it hadn't awakened me before the phone call. The answering service put me through to the hospital and I spoke with the nurse. We discussed and solved the problem, and I turned over to go back to sleep. At that instant, something fell, like "SLAM!" It startled me, but I was too sleepy to get up and check what happened. Besides, there wasn't anything on the walls that would fall like that and there was no sound like something had broken. I put the sound aside and fell back to sleep.

When I awoke in the morning, I got out of bed and started to get ready for the day's work. As I walked around the bed, it occurred to me that something had fallen during the night. I looked on the floor around the bed and then on the wall where there were some pictures. Everything was in place. Then I happened to glance at the top of the bookcase. The lamp was fine. But the book of poems was flat down on its back on the bookcase, with the front of the book facing upward looking to the ceiling. I thought, "That's strange. The past four years I had that special book of poems on its edge with the leaves wide open. It had never fallen flat down in all that time, not in any way."

This book of poems by Helen Steiner Rice had been one of my Eileen's favorite poem books. She read it almost every night before going to sleep. Even though I was there with her most nights, I never really noticed the title of this book. I picked it up and actually, for the first time, noticed the title, *Someone Cares—The Collected Poems of Helen Steiner Rice* (see photo).

I immediately perceived the deep meaning and message and held the book close to me with a touch of magic filling my heart and tears of joy welling up in my eyes. As I slowly came to the truth of it all, I gave the reality of it the final and human test. I put the book on the shelf on its edge <u>exactly</u> as it had been for the past four years. Then I started to shake the bookcase, at first gently, and finally vigorously. Everything on the shelf shook and jarred, except the book of poems, which stood there as stable as the Rock of Gibraltar. I tried pushing it down and I could plainly see, even with my pushing, that it would not have fallen flat—"SLAM"—as it did. It might have fallen against the wall or against the lamp, or totally off the bookcase. However, it would not have fallen back—"SLAM—on its back cover as it did! But that's exactly what happened.

Every day since that "coincidence" I have tried to shake that poem book down, and it has not fallen, although all of the bric-a-brac shakes quite easily, ready to topple unless I stop!

When I look back at that night, I can clearly understand that my Eileen picked the most appropriate time to "SLAM" the poem book down on its back cover. I was awake from the phone call and therefore would hear her "slam" telling me, "I'm thinking of you and I love you." The previous week had been particularly lonely and I was filled with self-pity. My Eileen picked a perfect way to comfort me.

Oh, by the way: I looked through this book of poems for the first time, and on one of the back pages is a poem *This I Believe*. My girl had bracketed a few lines – and <u>nowhere</u> else in this book:

And while man's motives and mission,
his programs and projects, and his
accomplishments and acclaim
can make him successful and secure,
for him a listing in "WHO'S WHO," he
remains unlisted in God's "WHO'S WHO."
For great is the power of might and mind,
but only LOVE can make us KIND...and
all we are or hope to be...is empty pride
and vanity...if LOVE is not a part of all...
the GREATEST MAN is very small!

Our love for each other is truly an example of this poem.
My Eileen was a woman of infinite care and love.

Eileen's poem book where it stood
on the bookshelf for four years

Eileen's poem book as it slammed
down one night on the bookshelf

The next two happenings occurred years apart to members of my family. The first one I will describe occurred to my sister-in-law Ann, a caregiver who was attending to an elderly couple in their home. It was a few years ago when cantankerous Hans was slipping steadily toward his future; not expected to live very much longer. Ann tells me he was an intelligent man who enjoyed a heated discussion. He had little faith in the "hereafter" and strongly proclaimed, "When you're dead, you're dead!" As he became weaker, Ann would sit with him, hold his hand, and try to comfort him. She was there night and day. He was particularly ornery during the night and would wake her over and over again for trivial things, such as, "Move the night table closer to the bed," when it was already as close to the bed as possible.

One night at about 4:00 a.m., Hans rang the bell for Ann after having called her many times during the night. Ann tells me she was so tired and irritated when she came down to him for some frivolous request, she "blew her top" and yelled, "Hans, you have everything you need and I'm dead tired. Don't keep calling me for no good reason." Well, this didn't decrease the night calls very much, but as Hans became weaker and weaker, Ann spent more time with him. He insisted to the very end against Ann's prayers and comforting help, "When you're dead, you're dead!" Hans died shortly thereafter and Ann continued to care for his companion, Caroline.

It wasn't two weeks later that precisely at 4:00 a.m. one day Ann was awakened by a loud and constant buzzing. She ran downstairs and found the oven buzzing away as if she had been roasting a turkey and it was cooked. She had to fiddle and fiddle with the switch to finally stop the buzzing. Then Ann smiled to herself and thought, "Hans is saying hello to me from the hereafter!" About a week later, Ann was sleeping peacefully when again at 4:00 a.m. the oven began buzzing. Ann ran downstairs and again had to fiddle and fiddle with the switch to stop the buzzing. This time with a smile, Ann said, "Hans, I know you are up there and you are all right. Please don't wake me anymore." That was the last time the buzzer went off.

You must, of course, understand two things about this oven that Ann had learned:

(1) The oven switch doesn't work!

(2) During all her time there, the oven had <u>never</u> buzzed! Hans changed all that!

&ᾱ &ᾱ &ᾱ

On December 3, 1963, my Eileen delivered our fourth child and second son in a small hospital in Cornwall, New York. It was a great occasion for us, as he was strong and healthy. And Jimmy has been a great pleasure to us ever since.

This same year, 1963, however, had a very dark side to it, especially for my Eileen. That year, Eileen's Mom, Grandma McVeigh, was dying of terminal cancer of the pancreas. All our children were very young then, as were Jim McVeigh's children. Jim McVeigh is Eileen's brother, and he and his family lived near us in Poughkeepsie. Something very special happened one morning when Jim's daughter, Cathy, was not yet four years old and our Jimmy was in his third week of life. During the early morning hours of December 19th, Cathy called to her mother Ann with an outburst of hysterical sobbing. She screamed to Ann, "Grandma is over there," pointing to the corner of the bedroom. "She's pointing at me and saying, 'You be a good girl.'" Of course, Ann did not see anything, and it took her some time to help Cathy calm down. Cathy finally fell back to sleep in Ann's arms. Ann did not know what to make of all this. Later that morning, Jim McVeigh called his wife and told her that Grandma McVeigh had died early that morning, December 19th. When Ann and Jim compared "notes," they found that Grandma had died at precisely the very moment when she was visiting little Cathy. If you knew Grandma McVeigh, a caring and loving woman, this is exactly what she would tell her little Cathy as she was passing by on her way to a beautiful life in the next world.

ᏜᏜ ᏜᏜ ᏜᏜ

My sister Nancy told me about an unexplainable experience which happened to her a few years after our own Mom died. I have read and heard about such happenings, but Nancy had never known about anything like them. This is what she described to me:

One morning when she was in her bedroom combing her hair and making herself presentable, she was looking into the vanity mirror. Suddenly our Mom appeared in the mirror. Nancy was startled and incredulous. She moved her head from side to side, thinking this was some kind of reflection. But Mom was definitely standing there in the mirror. She wasn't smiling, didn't say anything, but looked serene and contented, seeming to indicate that she was all right. Her image then faded away. Nancy was definitely surprised, but quite aware that what had happened is exactly what happened.

Now, guess what? It was not a week later when Nancy was in the bathroom combing her hair while looking into the bathroom mirror. Suddenly Mom again appeared in the mirror. And again, Nancy moved about, incredulous at Mom's image, but she was definitely there, looking calm and serene. Then, without even a wave, Mom went away.

It is now a few years since, but Nancy hasn't forgotten seeing Mom in a mirror—twice. She still doesn't know what to make of it.

For those of you who might be interested in learning more about such perplexing spiritual experiences, I refer you to the most exciting book on the subject, *Reunions* by Raymond Moody, M.D.

꧁ ꧁ ꧁

Do you have that sixth sense? Intuition, we call it. We all do! Some of us are overflowing with it. But many of us see these "sparks of knowing" like "Oh, yeah," only at unexpected times. We pay no heed to them, passing them off as coincidence or recognizing for an instant something quite unusual. We can't explain it, but for whatever reason, we let it slip through our fingers, like water from a faucet. We refuse to take the time, refuse to let our minds grab onto it and sift it, examine it, and embrace it, probe it to its very depth. This is too wonderful, too impossible, too significant, too dangerous. It is more than we are ready or willing to honor or accept. And maybe that's why our intuitive power is not overflowing in many of us. We refuse to bring ourselves to the reality of the unknown!

However, all of us know of or have heard of people with this immense sixth sense. Some of us have relatives or friends whose intuitive gifts (psychic powers) are plain and simply THERE to see, true and undeniable—even if we refuse to acknowledge such things.

Wonderful and exciting intuitive gifts have been occurring to people down through the ages, from Appolonius of Tyana, to Emanuel Swedenborg, the brilliant scientist and amazing mystic of the 1700s, to Edgar Cayce, the simple country boy, whose uncanny powers baffled and overwhelmed doubters during the early 20th century, to the most recent saint-to-be, mystic and miracle-worker Padre Pio who died in 1968.

During my life and work I have been privileged to know some gifted people who accept this immense wonder and sometimes burden with humility, grace, and peace of mind. I would like to tell you about Mary, a nursing supervisor, mother, and friend of many years. Mary didn't one day blurt out to me, "Hey, Doc, I often know things that are going to happen BEFORE they happen." No! We talked about my plans for a book since my beautiful Eileen's death and all of the special and unexplainable things that happened to me. And my total faith in my knowing—no doubt—that I would be with "my girl" again someday. Mary validated the unknown to me in her quiet and reassuring manner. She told me that as far back as she could remember, as a child, she knew certain events would occur before they happened. She couldn't tell anyone, since such things were not discussed at home. Maybe, Mary indicated, it was due to the fact that her grandmother had this same ability—and she was considered to be a "little" abnormal. Mary has a son and a daughter, and her daughter has this same ability. (I prefer to call it a gift.)

Mary recalled that at the age of five or six years, she was with her babysitter and was very restless and couldn't get to sleep. She told her babysitter that she just knew something was wrong with her mommy and daddy. During that night they received a phone call that Mary's mother and father had been in a car accident. Mom and Dad had not been seriously injured.

Mary was engaged and in college when her boyfriend's parents took a trip upstate to meet her parents. Mary told me, "Somehow, I knew deep down inside me that his mother would never return home. She was a healthy woman and had worked Saturday night. Sunday, she became ill while visiting and suddenly had a stroke. She was taken to the local hospital and died during the week.

About six or seven years ago when Mary was driving

home from work, she had a sudden alarming feeling: "My uncle is going to die!" She said to herself, "Why am I thinking this?" He was not sick or expected to die, however he died suddenly that very week.

Mary told me that she has had various premonitions during her life, some more ordinary. However, these have especially impressed themselves in her heart.

She told me of one other experience and feeling that occurred involving the father of her sister-in-law. He had been diagnosed as having cancer, but he was doing fairly well. Mary stated that "at some point, I knew he was going to die and very soon." He died that day.

Mary is a beautiful young woman. She leads a happy and joyful life and has given me much encouragement and understanding about the reality of the unknown.

The NDE

Anyone who has watched TV talk shows over the past few years is sure to have heard of another kind of death experience, which is called the "Near-Death Experience," or NDE. About thirty years ago this term was presented to the world by Dr. Raymond Moody, one of the original researchers on the subject who had the ability and courage to dig deeply into this phenomenon.

I had the pleasure of interviewing two young women who had near-death experiences. Before I present these NDEs to you, I would like to describe in general this phenomenon from many discussions and readings on this subject.

Near-death experiences, possibly a keyhole view of life after death, could be summarized as follows: Persons who are clinically dead are resuscitated, returning to life often almost miraculously. Some have been brain dead for so long that doctors expect them to return as "vegetables," or their bodies have been covered with a sheet and are in the morgue when they awaken.

After returning to life, they have amazing accounts of their experiences. Commonly they describe such phenomena as leaving their bodies and rising toward the ceiling of the room; remembering in minute detail everything that went on during the resuscitation, even from other rooms, such as the waiting room.

They may rise through a tunnel toward a bright light. They may meet a being of light who exudes such unconditional love that they never want to leave. Some see deceased friends and relatives. Some experience a complete review of their lives down to the smallest detail.

Many describe the most beautiful and vivid colors, music, and scenery. They may reach a river, hill, fence, or door, realize they can go no further and find themselves whisked back into their bodies, feeling the pain and reality of their condition. Many wish they hadn't returned to this life. Long-term after-effects are often significant, including no fear of death, a diminished interest in material possessions, and a deeper spiritual feeling.

Those interested may want to explore the evidence. I suggest the following references: *On Death and Dying* by Dr. Elizabeth Kubler-Ross; *Life After Life* by Dr. Raymond Moody; and *We Don't Die* by Joel Martin and Patricia Romanowski.

ও্ক৺ ও্ক৺ ও্ক৺

On October 17, 1998, I spoke with Ms. Evelyn Charter, and I now present her interview in its entirety, in her exact words:

I had a near-death experience in 1974, I believe. The reason that I was in the hospital:

I was going down for an exam, cystoscopic, where they go into the bladder, and everybody scared me to death that it was going to be very painful, so I insisted to the doctor that I be out. And he said, "Nobody gets put out to have..." and I said, "Well, this one does because I'm very afraid. Everyone says it's very painful."

Now at the time I only weighed about 82 pounds. And I believe what happened was that they gave me too much anesthesia for my body weight. That's the only thing I can think of, because you're certainly not going to have anything happen just from the exam. So I believe that that's the reason for it.

So I went in, had the exam, and it was when they had brought me back from recovery, and I remember being in the room, and there was a nurse taking my blood pressure, and I was observing this. I was observing this. I was like looking at me.

Dr: You were...

I was looking down.

Dr.: You were out of your body at that time.

Yes. And she was taking my blood pressure; she would pump it up, she would release it. She would pump it up again, she would release it. And she stopped doing that, went out of the room to the Nurse's Station. And this is how I know I was observing it, because I saw her leave the room, go to the Nurse's Station.

Dr.: You could see the Nurse's Station.

Yes.

Dr.: From above?

Yes.

And what it was like, it was like you had built a model and taken off the roof. So she went to the Nurse's Station and she said to the nurse, "I can't get a blood pressure reading on the patient in Room – and I have no memory of the room number. Room—whatever."

Dr.: You heard her say that.

Yes.

The other nurse and her both ran down the hall into my room and once again they were doing the blood pressure. Now, meanwhile, when they were running down the hall and maybe before they started doing my blood pressure again, what happened was, it was almost like I was on a conveyer belt, because I wasn't walking, but I was moving towards, so almost like on a conveyer belt, towards this brilliant light.

Now, not a blinding light when you look up at the sun, and you know, you squint. It was just a brilliant light that didn't bother your eyes or anything like that. I don't know how else to describe it. The most brilliant light, I don't think that you would ever see anything on earth like this. I was moving towards this light in what seemed to be like a narrow area, and there was light all over, but there was more light at the end of this. And I'm moving towards it, and without speaking, sort of like a telecommunication, this communicated to me like, "Are you ready?" That's it. Not any religious thing, or anything like that. Just, "Are you ready?" And with that I said, "What about the baby?" Because my youngest son was maybe 3 ½ years old, and I remember my mind wanting to go towards the light, but afraid about what would happen with my baby? Who would take care of my baby? I remember that being a thought, and as soon as I communicated, "What about my baby?" I started backing away from the light. There was nothing more communicated. There was nothing like, "All right," or anything like that. It was just, I went back, backwards away from the light. And that is probably when the head nurse was taking my blood pressure, and she said to the other one, "I have a reading; it's very low." She said, "We'll try it again." She tried it again and she said, "Yes, it is getting higher." And she said, "I think everything will be all right."

Now the most amazing thing about this? I had no memory of this until about a month later. I was on the phone with my sister-in-law and this happened up in Northern Dutchess Hospital, and at that time they had renovated. They had done the rooms over and they were done very nice. They were a light green with like a flowered green drapery. Very, very nice. And I was on the phone with my sister-in-law and we were speaking about how nice the rooms are there. And she said, "Yeah, I like the green, the light green." And all of a sudden it came to me in my mind, everything was white. And I said, "Green?" And she said, "Yeah, the green. You were just in there. Didn't you..." And I got right off the phone and I said, "Let me call you back." And I hung up the phone and that's when I got the memory of what had happened. And it was only because when I was looking down, everything was white. The floor was white, the walls were white. Everything was white. It was white. There was no color. And that must have triggered the memory of this. And I sat on my bed, and I'm thinking, "Did I dream this?" And I would go over it and over it and over it. And I said,

"Why am I thinking this?" You know?

And then maybe a year later I was reading a magazine and there was an article, and I said, "My God, that's what it was." I just didn't realize it. But it was amazing that I didn't in the hospital, I didn't wake up and say, "My God, look what just happened to me?"

So, and then another thing that I've always thought of. Since I remembered it, it didn't make me religious, but it did make me very spiritual. I don't go to a specific church and this and that and the other thing. I started praying, and I started feeling that there really is something more.

Dr.: Did you notice any other changes?

The only other thing that I always think about is that I don't have any fear of dying, because, if that's what it's like. Now, I don't know what would have happened if I didn't say I wasn't ready, or what about the baby. That I don't know. But since then, I've felt, it can't be that bad. Because I didn't think of it like a bad experience. And when I was moving towards the light, there wasn't any fear. There wasn't any fear like, "Oh my God, what is going on, or what is this?" It was just like moving towards it. It was almost like a peaceful sort of thing.

So that's my story.

Dr.: How old were you when you had this?

27.

Dr.: Then you came out of that and you were all right.

Yes.

Dr.: That's wonderful. Your son is grown up and you have your granddaughter?

Well, I have three sons. My oldest son is 31. He was around eight at the time of this. My middle son is 26. He was the one that was the little one. And my youngest son is 22. And the 22-year-old is the one with the daughter.

Dr.: Did you tell this to anyone else?

I have. But people... I find that people are like, "Yeah, right." Or when you try to explain it, people don't want to hear about things that seem out of the ordinary or supernatural. I have a sister-in-law who is born-again Christian, and she didn't think that it happened, because she thought that it would be more of a religious sort of thing, that the being would have said more about this, that, or the other thing. But I can't help what happened. That it was not religious or not, or whatever.

Dr.: Some people have a religious experience when they have a near-death experience. They have the sense that there's a being, and they're talking to someone. But others have one like yours, that it's just a peaceful, wonderful kind of experience and they're not afraid. That's what most people have.

Sure.

Dr.: Now tell me, you have a sixth sense?

I feel not that I'm psychic or anything, but certain things, I'll know that they're going to happen before they happen. And I'll wonder if that like connects in with that.

Dr.: Did you have anything like that before this experience?

Not that I remember.

Dr.: Do you remember anything specifically when you've said to yourself, "I know that's going to happen."

Well, you know, when it first started was with my oldest son. We're very, very close. Very close. I could almost will him to call me if I needed to speak with him. He had moved to Florida for a while. And all I would have to do is think really hard about it, and the phone would ring and he would say, "What do you want, Ma?"

Different things like that, or say I'll be driving down the road, and it'll come in my mind, "I'll bet I'm going to see a deer." And I'll go around the corner, and there's a deer. Just little things. Nothing super. I don't get Lottery numbers or anything like that. I wish I did! But just little things. The phone will ring and I'll say, "I'll bet that's so and so," and I'll pick it up and there they are. Just little things like that.

And that night at 3:30 in the morning I woke up out of a sound sleep, felt like there was an elephant sitting on my chest. I could hardly breathe. I sat up in the bed, and my husband woke up and he said, "What's wrong?" I said, "My God, I can't breathe." And he said, "Do you want me to get you a drink of water or something? Are you all right?" And I said, "Yeah. I'm all right now." And I laid back down, and for whatever reason, started thinking about my brother. Six the next morning I got the phone call. He lived in Texas. Six in the morning I got the phone call that my brother had died. And I said, "When?" And they said, "Twenty after three."

All near-death experiences are not exactly the same. Most

of them capture a portion of the characteristics set down from research and many, many accounts of people who have had such experiences. They are from people of all walks of life, from the very religious to the agnostic and atheist, from the elite to the plain and ordinary, from the very young to the very old. They are doctors, lawyers, salesmen, teachers, judges, laborers, mothers, children—you name it. Someone just like you has had a near-death experience. These accounts are in general uplifting, exciting, and challenging.

꿍ꗞ꒭   꿍ꗞ꒭   꿍ꗞ꒭

Here is the second interview from a nurse, Sandra Alley, in her exact words. It was recorded on October 21, 1998:

In 1979 I was in Vassar Hospital for surgery, a partial hysterectomy, and because of two abscess wounds, one on the incision and one pelvic abscess, I went into post-operative toxemia. The abscess on the abdomen incision was found; the abscess on the pelvic area was not found. I continued to get sicker and sicker, and my temperature continued to go higher. From all that I can gather, I went into a septicemia and I went into cardiac arrest in my bed. I knew that something was happening. I knew that I was in trouble. I knew that I was probably dying.

My first experience while lying in bed was I realized I was in a great deal of trouble and I wasn't going to get the help that I needed, and I just began to pray very, very hard to please help me. God help me, because I do know I'm in trouble. And I was a nurse and I did know I was in trouble. I knew that I was losing consciousness. I knew that my body was slowly losing it. And the first thing I saw was a ball of light which I don't know whether I was awake or asleep.

The ball of light was sort of hovering in the air over my head, and it seemed to descend from the ceiling down to just before my face. A very bright light, an extremely bright light that moved. I thought, "Oh, no. This is really it." And I can't say again whether I was conscious or not. The ball of light went away from my face, back up in the air near the ceiling, and I continued to pray very hard because I was very frightened. The ball of light again came to my face and continued to spiral in front of my face, and then the next thing that I realized, I was somewhere else. I can't tell you where I was, because I don't know where I was. I was in a, to me, in retrospect, I was in a another plane, I was in a different place, I was in a space that was, if you look at a beautiful sunny day and you see these wonderful clouds, puffy clouds of sort of white and gray and pink, and you see the rays of sun coming through the clouds. This was my environment. It was very misty, and way off in the distance, looking ahead, was this wonderful ray of light coming through this cloudy mist. And I was moving toward this light. I can't tell you that I was walking. I can't tell you that I was a body. I can only tell you that whoever, whatever form I was in, I was moving forward toward this light, and the feeling at this time was of immense, immense joy, immensely peaceful. The peacefulness was something that I had never experienced. I can't even describe it. But it's a supreme feeling of peace, joy, completely surrounded by, it's almost like you're enveloped in a sense of wonder and a sense of love, absolute love. When you hear the people describe, maybe in the scriptures, this absolute love, well this is the real thing. This is what you felt. You felt this absolute love and joy and peace. You weren't afraid. You're absolutely not afraid. You're just so happy to be there, and you're just overjoyed with this love and caring. I wish I could give you the words, but there are no words. There are no earthly words. I continued to move forward toward the bright light and was so happy that I was moving forward, and I could hear someone talking to me. But it's not like somebody standing in front of you talking to you. It's more like a mental telepathy kind of thing. It was all mental. Saying all was well and I was doing fine. And I thought, "Gee, this is wonderful. I wonder who this is talking to me." I had no idea, but I could hear these words of someone trying to add to my feeling of safety and love and peace and joy, which is exactly what it did. And I continued forward, and I just kept moving slowly toward the light, and I got closer and closer with this wonderful feeling. Then I heard someone say, "You have to go back." I don't know who it was; I don't know why. But the words came, "You have to go back... You have to go back, it's not time for you." And I was suddenly awake in my bed and the doctors and nurses were working on me and putting IV's in my arm, pumping on my chest, and all sorts of other things going on, and, of course, they rushed me back up to the O.R. at that time.

That was my experience. I can't say that when I woke up, it's like I was sleeping. But I wasn't sleeping. It was not a dream. It was not a hallucination. It was unexplainable and it took me quite a few months to digest what had happened to me. That I know it was not a dream, not a hallucination, and it certainly wasn't drug induced. And that's my story.

I was very angry that they made me go back.

Dr.: Oh yes, that's what they say.

I was very angry that I had come back and there I was. So I didn't add that.

Dr.: You didn't see yourself at any time, like went over to yourself and could see yourself?

No. I was just gone.

Dr.: Since your experience, after it's over, and you finally got well. Did you notice any change from the way you had been before this experience and after?

I think there's more of a general, there's more peace of mind. There's certainly no doubt that there is another life, and that there is somewhere that you go to, which is very comforting. I've always been a very accepting, liberal individual, but I think I've become even more accepting and more forgiving of people's foibles, and also that with this experience I think is the feeling that no matter who the person is, no matter what their thoughts are that are in their life, that they're going to be accepted into this wonderful, beautiful place. And, I mean certainly, I was not without sin and you hear if you're a sinner....but the feeling of forgiveness and the caring and the peace and the love is just so tremendous. It's not even questioned. You're just accepted into this peaceful, wonderful, joyful place. And you don't want to go. You just want to stay there and stay there.

You just want to be there. My thought also was that you become one with the universe. My own retrospective thinking about it is you're a body of energy. I think it's, maybe it's an energy of some kind, that your body turns into the light, that you become the light. That you become part of the light, and therefore the energy of life is in this light and that's why you're heading toward the light. That's my own thinking. Because you hear references over the years from different scriptures and literature, going to the light, the light. The light is always mentioned. To me the light became representative of the universe, and we in fact become part of the universe.

It doesn't matter who you are, it doesn't matter what you've done or not done. There you are.

When people say, "Oh, heaven, hell, all of this..." I can't go along with it. Because I know better. I know it's a very accepting place that you're going to go to.

Dr.: You don't have any real fear of death?

Absolutely not. I don't want to die. I want to live as long as I can live to enjoy my life here, but I know that when I die... In fact I've often said to my son, and thought of what I'd put on my gravestone, it's, "I'm in the light." So therefore, I'm still here.

Dr.: This is what we find, with so many people. It's a wonderful thing.

There's also a feeling that the light is there, and it's a very powerful feeling, but it's also that you know that the light is there, and you know that that power is there. You know it exists. There is no more doubt in my mind. In fact, this is what I get in arguments with my fellow nurses. Don't be so smug about it, girl, maybe that's not it. But I have to differ with them and say that this is it for me, and since I was there and you weren't, I can only tell you that if you had had the experience, that you would feel the same as I. And you would feel that there's a strength.

⚜ ⚜ ⚜

My daughter Theresa told me of this amazing encounter with a curve in a road:

One late afternoon, I needed to drive my daughter to her high school for band practice. My youngest daughter, then five, wanted to go along for the ride. So the three of us piled into my van and started off. I was pretty tired that day, not getting a good night's sleep the night before, but I didn't think much of it at the time. I did all right driving over the very curvy road on the way there, but on the way back, I started to really have to fight off the need to sleep. I had been tired before, but I had never come close to falling asleep while driving in my life before that day! There is one very treacherous hairpin turn on this road. It is distinctly marked well before you approach it, but the last thing I recall is seeing that sign with the "dangerous curve" arrow against the yellow background. The next thing I saw as I abruptly woke up was the big white house well after the hairpin turn. I had slept through the entire drive down the roadway and around that sharp turn! There would be NO WAY I shouldn't have crashed being asleep behind the wheel on that portion of the road. And I was most definitely not awake! I was startled and scared when I awakened and realized where I was. I pulled over, my heart racing, because I knew I hadn't been doing any of the driving for the past several minutes. I knew a miracle had just taken place for me and my little girl in the back seat. Every time I drive— very slowly—around that turn, I remember to thank God, all the angels involved, and my Mom for guiding the van that afternoon. We couldn't have made it without that Divine Intervention.

This next beautiful ADC speaks for itself! Here it is, in my friend Nancy Haas's own words, with her superb sketch:

My sister Ann and I grew up in a small town on the Oregon coast not far from our grandmother's house. Gramma has always been to me THE shining example (in addition to our children later) of the embodiment of unconditional love in my life. The gift of growing up with her was and is profound! We spent many hours at her knee, by her side, and in her heart.

When Ann and I were in our late teens and early 20s, we had a particularly close bond—the kind you hear of where we finished one another's sentences, picked up the phone and said, "Yes, I'll meet you..." before the phone had even rung and without ever having to identify one another, etc. ...People who knew us thought we were kind of strange sometimes but it all seemed quite natural to us.

During this time our grandmother died. She had been quite ill for five years, battling cancer. Our father called us from Oregon, first one, then the other. Then we called each other. Of course we knew who it was. We lit candles together and cried together, laughed about old memories and smiled together over the phone. The next day we got together and shared stories and special times and more tears. There was to be no funeral or memorial as requested by Gramma, so Annie and I created our own.

On the third day my little daughter and I were just sitting down to read a story when the candle I had lit for Gramma that morning suddenly popped! We looked up to see the top half of the candle lying on the table beside the other half still in the candleholder. The half in the holder was burning! And, the half that had broken off was, too—at both ends (see illustration). Just then, the phone rang!

I picked it up and said, "I think Gramma just crossed over!" My sister said, "Yes, so do I...but why do you think so?" I told her about the candle! Then she told me, "Just now a dove landed on my windowsill and stayed for the longest time. I have lived in lots of places, but I have never seen a dove 'til today. Then a second dove landed next to the first. They cooed to one another and looked at me. They were not at all afraid. After quite a while, they flew away together." We both fell silent for many minutes. Through tears and smiles, we silently sent love and thanksgiving to our grandmother, Mary Frances Walters Miller. And stood

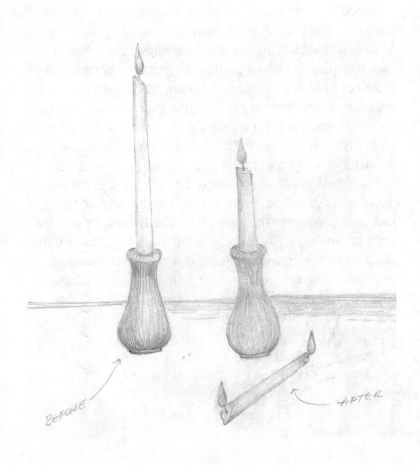

BEFORE

AFTER

Nancy Haas's drawing of her grandmother's candle

in the awe of human spirituality.

I still have that candle, wrapped and put away. My sister sees two doves outside her windows now, in her travels all over the world! We have both felt the presence of our grandmother at different times, just as though she were in the room with us. On one occasion, I experienced the most profound envelopment of love. As though I was being wrapped in a blanket. I smiled a deep inner smile and "hugged" her back! Then I received—not in spoken words, or in thoughts entering my mind somehow, but simply in an understanding, a knowing—that my grandmother and others were near me and completely willing and available to stay near me and help me in my life, like guardian angels, but if they were not needed, they would go on and further develop themselves. It was very clear that either way was fine with them and it was up to me!

I sobbed great tears! I loved having my grandmother near me in so-called death, loving me the way she always had, and reassuring me in my life. But I wanted more than anything in every fiber of my being to set her free! I wrote her a poem with tears streaming down my face and onto the page, assuring her, and me that I could do it! And that she was free to explore the vastness of her being. And I thanked her forever for everything that she is!

Nancy Miller Haas
April 16, 1999

CHAPTER
EIGHT

THE DEAD ARE ALIVE

*"There are more things in heaven
and earth, Horatio, than are
dreamt of in your philosophy."*

—*Shakespeare's* Hamlet

*"It is one of the commonest of
mistakes to consider that the
limit of our power of perception
is also the limit of all there is to
Perceive."*

—*C.W. Leadbeater*

"I haven't read this, so let me know what you think. Can't wait to have you out here! Love, Nick." With this note dated May 16, 1996, almost two months after my beautiful, wonderful Eileen was taken from me out of this world, I received a package with a book in it from our son,

Nick. Although within those two months after my Eileen's death my mind had been challenged, stretched, imploded by those events which I have described previously, I had not done any serious reading or investigations into the fact of after-death communications. However, this book entitled *We Don't Die* by Joel Martin and Patricia Romanowski, and another book entitled *Hello From Heaven* by Bill and Judy Guggenheim, stared me down the winding road to exploring the voluminous literature about parapsychology and my faith in the hereafter. *We Don't Die* is an amazing report on George Anderson's "conversations with the other side." By now, I have no doubt that many of you have heard of George Anderson. He has been featured on radio and television and has conducted numerous private and public readings, as well as having been tested by doctors, parapsychologists, and skeptics alike. No one has been able to explain his remarkable gift, nor has anyone found him to be anything but a sincere, honest, and spiritual individual. He is world-renowned for his genuine capabilities and his care and compassion for everyone.

After reading *We Don't Die*, I decided I must see George Anderson in person. The excitement of "possibly" making contact with my dearest love was more than I had ever dreamed could happen. I called George Anderson's office and spoke to his appointment secretary. It was now June 1996 and there were no available appointments until April 1997. So be it. I made arrangements for the consultation for my six children and myself. The date was April 16, 1997. The discernment was enormously satisfying and uplifting. I will describe much of it to you in detail and with corroborating and interesting family facts.

Before I describe this amazing event, please allow me to ask that you read about three other such discernments, perhaps as a validation of my own. I promise you will find reading them a delight, as well as informative.

The first one comes from the hand of Della, the sister of a missionary, priest, and friend of mine from California. He is Irish and his sister lives in Ireland. This is one of the most beautiful and heartwarming communications I have ever heard. Here is Della's story.

During Rian's Pregnancy

My experience was with a blind psychic while I was seven months pregnant with Rian. During my pregnancy with Rian, a friend and I decided to go to a local hotel one evening where a blind female claiming to be psychic was showcasing. Neither of us had an agenda and both of us were rather skeptical. I'm always wary of people who claim to have such gifts, and especially if there is money involved.

Much of the evening was spent with this woman calling out names and relaying messages from dead family and friends to people in the audience. While the people involved were showing very obvious signs of awe and amazement, I was still rather unimpressed and cynical. Then she called my friend's name and gave her a very special message for another friend from her dead father who had just died in a fire. Now I was impressed.

Towards the end of the evening, she invited people to come for "healing." This simply involved the woman placing her hands on people and telling them of very specific areas in the body/mind that needed healing, so I thought, "Why not?" When my turn came, she became agitated and confused and started talking beyond me (as if to someone else), stating that she was now healing and not wishing to connect with the "other side." But she continued by saying, "Your sister is here, and oh, she's so thin (which she was). She knows you're pregnant and wants to reassure you that she will be with you the day of the birth." She also told me that I was aware of the sex of the child (which I was, having previously had an ultrasound scan). I was quite calm but overwhelmed at the same time. I'd never expected anything like that to occur. I asked one or two silly questions in my confusion, whereupon the psychic said, "Sure isn't she there for you, as always," an expression Eithne always used with regard to me. She finished by telling me how Eithne had died of a brain hemorrhage and had herself been a healer, and reassured me that Eithne was fine.

During Rian's Birth

It's fair to say that my experience of Rian's pregnancy was a happy and healthy one, physically and psychologically. I felt great. Life was very full around that time (December 1996). We were putting an extension onto our house and I had all the usual duties of a mother of two young daughters as well as lecturing once, sometimes twice a week, right up to and after Rian's birth.

By gestation week 32 the baby's head was shown to have engaged in the pelvis—a condition often thought to lead to a premature birth. In fact, Rian, who was due on the first of December 1996, didn't arrive until 10:35 a.m. on the sixth of December. On a personal and emotional level, there was no doubt I was painfully aware of my sister Eithne's absence (by her death on January 1995). She was my older sister, my confidant, and my rock in times of crisis. I was also saddened that just as my other two children would grow up without knowing her loveliness, this new little life would also be denied such a beautiful person.

During the early hours of the fourth of December, I felt the first signs of regular, painful contractions. By virtue of this being my third experience of labor, I knew I had many hours to go before the birth, so I proceeded to keep myself as mobile and busy as possible, which included going into town (Cork City) to do the Christmas shopping.

It wasn't until 6 a.m. on the sixth of December that I decided I needed some form of pain relief, so with the help of a female companion, I summoned a taxi and went to the hospital. Up to this, I had paced the sitting room floor, with a tissue soaked in lavender oil for comfort. I reminded myself that it was my sister Eithne who had introduced me to aromatherapy, and she referred to lavender as her "medicine chest in a bottle." Once in the hospital I felt out of control, alone, scared, and now very much in pain. After the routine examinations I was left alone with my tissue for comfort. As I have a history of slow labors, the staff were inclined to suggest acceleration in the form of an Oxytocin drip. From previous experiences, I had already decided that this was not an option and I very much wanted to deliver the baby at my own pace.

By 9:45 a.m. I was informed that I was only 4 cm dilated (with 10 cm being necessary for delivery). This was very disheartening and the staff again began to organize a drip. Somehow, from deep within myself, I yelled, "No," and began the process of pushing. I felt completely in control and ready for the birth of my baby. Having been sitting on a chair, I climbed onto the bed, in order that the nurse could examine me. Much to her amazement, she could see the baby's head. Surrounded by the smell of lavender, I continued to push. This stage of labor is often the most painful and distressing for many women, but to my amazement, I felt relatively at ease.

Meanwhile, panic was beginning as the midwife was now aware that this baby was going to be born on the bed in the labor ward and not in the delivery room. They asked me to stop pushing for a moment while they got their gloves, etc. This I did with ease. I was at this stage very calm, relaxed, and in total control; these details are noteworthy when one considers that this is possibly the most painful phase of childbirth (i.e.: just before birth). I lay on my left side, surrounded by a soft, white light, aware that the staff were beginning to panic, but completely oblivious to their fears. As Rian entered this world, a voice kept reassuring me that "It's okay, Della. This one has a helping hand into the world." It was Eithne's voice and she was there to my left by my head. I never at any stage saw a figure. It was simply the most overwhelming sense of her presence. My partner later informed me that I smiled all the way through the birth of the baby's head. For my part, I was unaware totally of the pain of delivery, and felt myself to be floating in the whiteness that engulfed me.

After the birth (as any mother will confirm) there is the most amazing rush of endorphins and exhilaration. Sadly, I missed those first few moments of bonding with the baby as I refused to accept that the experience was over, and knew that once I opened my eyes and acknowledged the baby, Eithne was gone. Eventually, with tears in my eyes, I looked at the baby. Much to the confusion of my partner and the staff around me, I explained to my partner, Brendan, that I was communicating with Eithne and that she was now gone again.

꒰ꙆꙌ   ꒰ꙆꙌ   ꒰ꙆꙌ

This second story will only enhance your understanding and belief in discarnate communication. This comes from Al Beres, who is one of the most honest and caring men I know.

Al's Story

Susan VanVlack went with me to see George Anderson on February 2, 2000. Of course, the talk on the drive down was almost never-ending. We both had a lot of preconceptions about what might occur at the discernment. Most of the conversation was about just what would happen with respect to me, not Susan. She had joined me for the appointment as a precaution so that she could drive back in the event that I needed someone to do so. She did not go with any expectation of participating in the spiritual communication; in other words, she was mostly along for the ride. When we got to our appointment, we were pleasantly surprised with fresh-baked cookies and coffee. We arrived an hour early, which allowed us even more time to contemplate what might happen. Our conversation was mostly of how would I know these communications would be real? How would I know that the spirits were who they said they were? So, I began to mentally round up my friends and relatives who had passed away. I also began to put them in a sort of order of probability of showing up. We sat down with George, who began the discernment with his customary prayer and a signing of the cross. I was very surprised when he immediately directed his communication from the other side not to me, but to Susan, whom George knew absolutely nothing about. After all, her presence was the result of a last-minute decision. I could see that she was getting very emotional, but I of course didn't fully understand because I knew nothing of the spirits coming through for her.

Sue recalls, "The first thing he said to me was, 'Does the name Margaret mean anything?'" It did. Margaret was Susan's mother's sister, her aunt. However, Susan merely nodded yes. Margaret had a message for Susan's mother. She asked that Susan tell her hello for her, and said she would see her (Susan's mother) "on the other side."

Susan's aunt was the first of several people she would encounter. George said to Susan, "Jim, Jimmy—do you understand?" Susan was puzzled, and looked at me. George said it again, "Jim, Jimmy—I'm getting Jim, Jimmy. Do you understand?" Susan realized it was her next-door neighbor,

Jim, who had died approximately twelve years earlier. Only two weeks before, Susan had visited Jim's grave and had jokingly suggested to Jim, out loud, that he show up at the discernment and say "howdy" (he was a Texan). Susan didn't even know that she was definitely going at that point. George said, "He (Jim, Jimmy) is not a relative, but he looks at you with great love and wants to thank you for always being his friend."

After this, George directed communications to Susan from two men who were standing behind her. Oddly, both men claimed to be her dad, a mystery cleared up because one was her biological father and the other was her stepfather. Through George, each communicated private and highly personal information to her. Susan's ex-husband George, whom I also knew, came through with some of his idiosyncratic, sarcastic humor. A recently deceased sister-in-law, whose death was known only to Susan's immediate family, also spoke through George Anderson.

George, at some point, directed what was happening toward me. He said, "There's a fatherly figure coming through. Recently deceased? Do you understand?"

I did, indeed, and I responded with an emphatic *yes* nod.

"He wants you to know that although your relationship was not what it should have been, he did love you in his own way," continued George.

He was also able to bring my mother through for me, telling me, "She is over there and on the vacation she never had on this earth." My grandmother was with her, and that too was confirmed by what she had to say.

There were other family members that would come through, but my mother stepped back in with a few words for Susan: "I just wanted you to know that I was not ignoring you while I was talking to Al." She wanted to acknowledge Susan's presence. Susan and my mother had an interesting relationship while my mother was here on earth. The events thus far would have sufficed to validate the reality of spiritual communication, but what would follow would, as someone once said, seal the deal for me.

As the discernment went on, I continued to mentally place people in a tentative order of arrival. My cousin Frank, U.S. Marine Corps, would, I thought, be the last. He survived World War II on Iwo Jima and Okinawa, only to die tragically in a car accident in 1962. The next thing George said was, "There's someone here who wants to know if there's someone waiting for him to show up: 'Is there anyone here waiting for me?'" These words were straight from my cousin, through George, and I knew it. I was stunned and overcome with emotion. George said, "He also wants to thank you for taking care of him," and I also knew what that meant, too, and now I know that Frank knows. George then said, "I have a Bill or a William coming through. No, not Bill or William: Bill William. Do you understand?"

I nodded a *no*. I didn't know who it was at the moment. Then George said, "Well, in any case, he's there on the other side, hanging out with your dad." George then said that spirit presences were ending their communications.

George, Susan, and I had a sort of off-the-record, no-spirits-involved conversation. George asked Susan some questions at first and then talked to me. He wanted to know if I had made any sense out of the "Bill William" who showed up.

In the interim, I had put it together. While I didn't know a Bill William, I was very familiar with the name Billy Williams, although I hadn't spoken the man's name in thirty years. He was a man my father worked with in the years immediately following World War II. The two of them got along very well in that they both liked to sing. Billy Williams went on to become famous in the recording business. His version of "I'm Gonna Sit Right Down and Write Myself a

Letter" was a top-ten hit in the late fifties. Now Billy Williams, my father, my mother, and my cousin Frank are all there. They are not dead, and I am convinced of this.

I hope everyone who has the need to see someone like George, as I did, finds an opportunity. There is a God, one God, and this whole experience was part of God.

Al Beres and I became good friends over the short space of a year's acquaintance. We met at the Barnes and Noble Bookstore when we were both looking for the same book by George Anderson. He is well aware of my many experiences since my Eileen's death. We believe she sent <u>him</u> a loving message for my daughters and me. Here it is in Al's words.

When the Molley family invited me to join them at their annual get-together, I jumped at the chance. It was at a place called Winterclove, which was new to them and certainly to me. I had never been in that section of the mountains before, and getting there took a little doing. It was out of the way, although not that far from where I lived, a very nice, old-fashioned hotel.

I had called in advance to check that a room was reserved for me. While on the phone, the clerk assured me that one was: room number 16. When I got to the front desk to check in, the clerk said that room 16 was already occupied, and while she didn't know how that had happened, would I be willing to take another room. Of course I would, I responded. After a little deliberation, the clerk realized that the second choice room was also occupied. Finally she said, "We only have one room left." While it was on the same floor as the rest of the family's rooms, it was unfortunately on the other side of the hotel. It was okay with me. I headed up the staircase, and about halfway up, something caught my eye. On my left and above me was a towel closet doorway.

The door itself was not so special, but what was hanging on it was. It held a plaque not found outside any of the other rooms, including my original reserved room, number 16. Written on the plaque were the words, *Bless My Ladybugs*. Hanging from the plaque's bottom were three carved wooden ladybugs. The plaque was about three feet from room 4, and there were no other plaques anything like this anywhere else in the hotel. The plaque reminded me of what Joe Ross had once said about his wife Eileen and the endearing name she had for their three daughters, *Ladybugs*. I took some pictures of the plaque (see photo) I had to let Joe know about this experience of mine, but waited to have the film developed so that he could also see what I saw there. I subsequently met with Joe and gave him the pictures.

A long time ago, I worked as a milkman's helper, delivering milk up and down some god-awful stairs in Brooklyn. I swore I would never make another delivery of any kind ever again. Well, now I've gone back on that oath with this very special message from Eileen to Joe and their family.

Plaque on Al Beres's hotel door

Eileen with her "ladybugs"
From left: Eileen Ann, Eileen, Theresa, and Nancy

᠀᠀᠀   ᠀᠀᠀   ᠀᠀᠀

This third discernment from Kim O'Brien is an amazing "down to earth" discussion of her talk with George Anderson. As you will see, Kim's new tape recorder didn't work, so this is an "off the cuff" interview from her notes.

September 9, 1999

This is Kim O'Brien speaking about her experiences with George Anderson.

I brought a brand new radio with a tape recorder in it, brand new tape, batteries, everything for this meeting. And the girl that went with me, Amy, tested it out to make sure that it worked. But then we went in there for our meeting and the tape did not tape at all. All the tape was static. So I believe that Danny did that for a reason, because he knew that I would sit there and listen to it over and over.

But George started out the meeting. He said that a young woman and two men came in. I didn't recognize the young woman, so he went on from there. He said one man passed on young for today's standards, not a boy but young, and I knew immediately he was talking about Danny. George says he feels pain in his chest and in his head, like something was exploding, the heartbeat was irregular, he felt like he was suffocating, and kept saying, "I get a falling, I'm falling." Which I believe Danny did when he died because I remember his pointer finger was broken. I remember that. Because I came home and the way his hand was, it looked so uncomfortable, and I moved him and I knew it was broken. So he had to fall. Whether it was off the couch or he stood up, I don't know.

The girl that I went with, Amy, George pointed to Amy and he said, "He keeps calling you sister, but you're not really sister." He wants to thank you for all your support that you've given her, and he was talking about me, and he doesn't want you to feel ignored or left out, but he's been waiting a long time for this meeting. Then George turned to me and says, "This is so strange, because I was just playing this song last night, and it's from an opera, it's called *The Merry Widow* and he pointed right at me and said, "You're his widow, but you're not very merry." I said, "No, I'm not. You're right."

Danny keeps putting a valentine heart over me and you're definitely his wife. What else? Oh, Danny kept showing George the Blessed Mary and he says that you're not a religious family but you keep praying to him in your own way and you keep sending him prayers. Which is true. I believe in God. I believe in life after death. But I don't go to church on a regular basis and that's just me, that's just the way we were. But we do pray to Danny; I do say the rosary for Danny. Because I believe that he gets it. And I believe that it does help them.

George said this a lot, and when I finish you'll understand why he said it so much. George says, "He keeps handing you stuffed animals." He said, "You have a stuffed animal collection from him." Which I do. And George looks at me and says, "Now I know why I got what I got today, but we'll do that later." That kind of piqued my interest. Danny kept handing me flowers; he kept handing me white roses for our anniversary, which is in October, which is next month.

He says that he's glad that if one of us had to go it was him, because he wouldn't make a good widower. Which is true. George says that he wanted me to know that he didn't suffer, that it was quick, and that he didn't feel any pain, that there wasn't anything that could have been done to save me, meaning Danny. And those were my big questions that I went for. I know that you (interviewer) told me, but I wanted to hear it from Danny. And George said that even if I was home, it wouldn't have made a difference, it happened that fast. And I'm glad that it happened quickly, that he didn't suffer.

Danny said we had a good marriage, that we had our ups and downs but more good times than bad ones. He said that he knows that I love him and that he loves me too. And this is what got Amy, because she was very skeptical walking in there. She went with me; she didn't want me to get ripped off, so she says. And I said, "Believe me, I'm not getting ripped off. Not with George." And this is what really got her. George says, "Another male just came in and his name is Al. And Al says that Danny met him and welcomed him into the light, and Danny said that Al really livens the place up," which is true." And this is when George got Danny's name. He didn't have it until Al came in. And he said, "Al keeps pointing and saying, "This is Dan, Dan the man."" And I shook my head yes, and he said, "Now I understand why I keep hearing 'Oh Danny Boy.'" And I said yes, that's it. Now Al is a gentleman who died the same summer, the summer of '98, that him and Danny knew each other. And that's what got Amy, because she's like, well yeah, he could have investigated and found a lot of stuff, but how would he know that Dan and Al knew each other?" So, Dan says there was a large turnout for his funeral, which there was. Danny was... you wouldn't believe. The church, we had to set up chairs in the back, and it was a large Catholic Church, and people were still standing. What a tribute. I thought, what a tribute to him. I had people come up to me that I didn't even know and say, "Danny was so wonderful." But you're so lost at the time anyway. "Well I knew him at the Beverage Center" because he worked at the Beverage Center on the weekends, and he knew everybody, absolutely everybody.

Danny says that I need to take care of myself because there's a part of me that just doesn't, excuse my language, give a shit, which was true at the time. Danny tells George that if it weren't for the kids that I would have curled up and died, which is true. He makes reference to the stuffed animals again and then George says that this gives him the chills, and he says I'll explain it afterwards.

Danny called out to, specifically by name, his best friend from high school, Richie, his Uncle Mike and his brother John. He also called out to his parents and my parents, but not by name. He said that I need to move on with my life and be happy; that I need to get a job because I sit at home and obsess over his death, which at the time is true, but I don't do that any more. He says it was a sticky situation with his parents, which is true. It was always a touchy kind of feely thing. He hadn't seen his Dad in quite some time, the whole time we were together, which was ten years, it would have been ten years this year. He hadn't seen his Dad the whole time we were together, so...

He told George that I might get married again or be in a

situation like marriage. I shook my head no when he said marriage. Because I always said I'd do it once, only once, and that's it. This was funny. Danny called out to the girls and George says two children, both daughters, no one of each. No, no. Ok. Ok. Sorry, sorry. He's very adamant, you have two daughters. He's yelling at me. I didn't say one of each, I said two girls. So that got us because Danny was a very family-oriented person. His children, his daughters, that's what he always wanted. And he was on Cloud 9, and you just couldn't knock him off of that. You just couldn't. He said the girls feel like he abandoned them and I need to reassure them that he hasn't and that he, Dan, had George get something to prove to them that he will always be there for them. This is good, too. George says that Danny is always with us, that he has given me signs, that I have seen him and, "No, you weren't drunk." (Laughs) So that explains it then. I have seen Danny in the spirit state, and he looks the same as if he was sitting across from me. Wild. Absolutely wild. And that he comes to us in our dreams. He says, "Yes, I do come to you in your dreams." George says he holds an apple over my head and tells George that I was the apple of his eye. And he says that your marriage was good and that you were friends before anything, and he says that you were a wonderful wife and you didn't ask for anything and that little things always made you happy. Which is true. He'd bring me home a candy bar and that would make me happy. Because it was something that he got. That he thought about and got it for me. A pencil, whatever. It's something that he stopped and took the time to think about me. And that made me happy.

He keeps handing me flowers and stuffed animals—through the whole session he did that. He tells George that I must complete my lessons here on earth, that he knows it will be hard but I will do well. He says that I'm not sleeping well at night, which I wasn't at the time, but I think that was all working up to this meeting and being anxious. He says that I should not get upset when family try to give me advice. He met my great-grandfather on the other side. He says he's met a William on the other side but doesn't know him well. That's my great-grandfather. He only met my great-grandfather once before my grandfather passed away. So I'm assuming that's who it is.

Danny says that I need to be more careful with my driving, that I talk out loud to him too much and don't pay attention, which is absolutely true. It's so strange, I don't know why, but I'm always looking in the clouds for him. I'm always waiting to see him sitting in a cloud. I'm always waiting to look up and see him sitting on the edge of a cloud going "Here I am." It's so strange, but that's just me.

He was getting ready to leave, so he gave Amy and I hugs and sends his love, and Al sends his love and to tell his family that he's heard from us. Danny's last message was that he will be waiting for me and will welcome me into the light when it's my turn to pass on. Which is nice to know, that he'll be there. George liked Danny. He liked him. He says, "Danny's a very straightforward person. He tells it like it is even though sometimes it hurts people's feelings." And that Danny had a very good sense of humor. I said, "Oh yeah, that was him."

So after Danny and Al left, George got up and he went behind his chair – I should have brought it with me, I didn't think about it – he went behind his chair and he brought out a little stuffed teddy bear. And that's what Danny used to give me every Christmas. And it had a little red hat and a little red scarf on it, and the name of it is "Peppermint, Love Me True." And it's a TY, TY Attic Treasure. And I didn't start collecting Beanie Babies until after Danny passed away. So how could he know, you know. And he gave me a guardian angel plaque for the girls, and he said anytime the girls want to talk to their Dad, they just need to go to this and talk to him. It gives them an object to go to.

And that's about it. It was awesome. I would pay ten times that amount to go back again. Definitely. He is a true gift. He really is a true gift.

Interviewer: Was Amy convinced?

Kim: Oh yeah. She was crying just as hard as I. We weren't even five minutes into the reading and I cried through the whole reading.

Interviewer: I understand completely. So you're totally convinced that your husband is alive somewhere.

Kim: Oh yeah.

Interviewer: So am I.

The George Anderson Visit

On April 16, 1997, almost 13 months after my Eileen died to this world, my six adult children and I drove to Long Island to meet with one of the world's most well recognized mediums, George Anderson. His schedule was so full that from the time I had made contact with his office in June 1996, the first free time on his schedule was in April of 1997.

My youngest daughter Eileen wrote me a letter some time after I had told her of our appointment with George Anderson. I still have it—somewhere—but I can't find it among all the cards and letters that my 'kids' have sent me. However, I will try to paraphrase what she said to me about our coming visit to Mr. Anderson.

'Dad, I'm so happy that you made these arrangements for us. Even if Mom doesn't show up at the discernment, it will be such an exciting experience.'

Well, Mom did show up, and through George Anderson spoke to each one of us personally.

George Anderson is not an imposing figure of a man. He is small of frame and just average-looking, but he reflects a confidence and sincerity that makes it easy to relax and appreciate the wonders that come through him from your loved ones on the Other Side.

We were ushered into his office and, in fact, his assistant had to get a few extra chairs, since usually only two or three people attend a session. Mr. Anderson sat on a stool in front of us. He had a pad and a pencil and as he looked at us he said words to this effect:

I really won't be writing anything. However, I sort of doodle with the pad so as not to be constantly looking at you. I don't want you to feel that I am looking for clues. The thing is, this discernment is for you, and I am just the instrument.

I may announce something symbolic and you can say yes or no or I understand. Don't explain anything. This can be anybody's ballgame, and whom you least expect can show up: relatives, neighbors, friends—whether you know them personally, whether they passed on 50 years ago. And that's why I emphasize that you say yes, no, or I understand. Acknowledge that you know they are here and we can go on. They are going to be discerned in the manner that they think you know what they're talking about. So even if I don't understand what they are saying, they are going to expect you to understand. Remember to see things from their perspective. We can discuss it all later. I'll look away from you as I can better hear and feel their presence.

Now, I will try not to praise Mr. Anderson too much, but during the discernment he expresses his opinion of your loved ones as he sees them, and he is remarkably accurate in his description. I have found this to be true in many of his discernments that I have read, and he was very clear about our Mom. I will put his thoughts about her together. Possibly from what I have written about Mom you will see that he is very accurate in his awareness of her personality.

George Anderson said:

I am getting the impression that your mother had a good sense of humor, because as I am joking, it is part of her joking that her sense of humor is coming through to me.

And another time:

Your mother seems to have a profound personality. She seems to call a spade a spade. She is not a b.s. artist. She is not going to come in and candy-coat anything. She is obviously a very family-oriented woman.

And later on:

Your Mom is obviously a very spiritual individual. She is aware that you (Theresa) *brought her rosary with her, and she says, 'You can pray the rosary for me.'*

George Anderson began abruptly with:

Well, a female presence has come into the room. Two as a matter of fact. There's somebody else. And a male, and another male, and another female. Five people have come into the room so far. Two of the females claim to be two different generations. They talk about being family. Someone in the crowd is talking about that younger female that passed over. (Now, by today's standards, anybody from the 60s down, I consider young.) Now someone in the room is stating, 'Mom is here.' Something about a spousal loss. That's what she is saying. Wife and mom. Now she claims her mom is here. Also her dad. They also talk of loss of a brother. Now your mom claims she passes not long ago, because it seems like she just got there. Your mom also speaks of her in-laws as also here in the room. And of a sister-in-law.

Your mom speaks of a miscarriage. Because she is talking about 'there would have been the birth of another son.'

Wait a minute! I don't understand. One of you felt that you could not save her, because she keeps telling me to tell you it's not your fault that she passed on, because, she says, 'You could not save me.' I wonder what she's driving at. Oh, ok. Now I see she indicates you are a doctor and she is saying you took good care of her but you could not save her. But your wife says that first of all she hasn't died and one of these days, when you pass on, all of you, are going to see her again because you have no place to go but her front door.

She speaks of her illness and it sounds like it obviously affected a large part of her body. She keeps telling me she's walking fine.

And then—almost as an aside:

Also in the background, did somebody speak another language? It's like German or something in the background.

Note: Eileen's grandparents were German and Irish.

Then he goes on:

Your mom also claims she has come in dreams, because she states, 'This is not the first time you're hearing from me.' She says she has visited in dreams. She says that she's been very much near. Also, times you're thinking of her, a song comes on the radio that relates to her.

Then abruptly:

Did someone in the family speak Italian? It seems like I'm hearing that in the background now.

Note: My grandparents spoke Italian.

Anderson then goes on:

There is also talk of loss of a pet. I hear a dog barking. Your mother keeps talking of the pet dog that passed on is there with her. She states the animal was as much one of her children as the rest of you.

Note: Our dog was sick for about a year and Mom took especially good care of him. He was a gentle and loving dog, an Akita.

Wait a minute. I'm hearing Bill, William. Your mother says there are two of them. I get the feeling William is family.

Note: William McVeigh was Eileen's father.

But, she says Bill is very unique to the family. Oh, I get it. Bill is the dog. Your Mom talks about the animal hooking up with her. She claims that the animal is the first living thing to welcome her into the light. Because, she says, 'Bill wakes me out of the coma' by barking at her and she wakes up on the spiritual side when she wakes up, a bit apprehensive. And she states that Bill took any stress or fears away and it made the passing complete because he barked her into the light, where she then saw other relatives and friends waiting for her. Mom says that she's not surprised that Bill greeted her first; he was so happy to see her.

Bill in the backyard

With the mystery of George Anderson's gift of 'seeing and hearing' from the Other Side, we were presented with more specific conversations from relatives and friends, and especially from Mom. As George Anderson relates some of Mom's comments to us, someone else seems to pop in with a thought or an exclamation and I will interject these as they come to us.

My Eileen speaks to me a number of times through George:

Your wife says to you that a lot of times you just wish you would die. However, you still have a purpose here as an individual and she says when you do pass on, know that she will be there to welcome you.

All of a sudden, George interjects:

Wait a minute. Your Mom keeps bringing up a sister–calling out to her. 'Tell her you heard from me.' She just wants her to know she's all right.

Note: This is her sister Ann, who told me about Hans.

Again Eileen tells George about my moves. First, she wants me to know she has no problem with that. Then she says to 'watch where you are walking, especially on the stairs. Make sure you put the light on.'

Note: At this time, my son Jimmy was putting a second floor addition to his house for me and for a special master bedroom for him and his wife, with a Jacuzzi. The work was not yet completed, and I was still living in the little cottage. However, Mom must have already known, because she suggested I be careful on the stairs and put the light on. You can be sure I follow her advice.

These next remarks from Mom brought tears to my eyes because it was our last wonderful trip together just two weeks before she became so seriously ill. George states:

She is talking about a trip to Hawaii. It's significant to her. Apparently she was there just before she got ill. She keeps talking about a happy trip to Hawaii. She says by her talking to me about that trip that you'll know I'm hearing from her. She says, 'I'm fulfilling my part of the code.' Not that you planned a code, but you'll know what she means.

Mom speaks to my youngest daughter, Eileen. George directs his remarks to Eileen:

I keep seeing Walt Disney World. I keep seeing Cinderella's Castle, and your mother keeps wishing you a happy trip to what I'm seeing. Plus, your mother states you could use the vacation, because she puts clouds over your head that are beginning to break. Sometimes your mother is concerned about your being alone. That at times you have the greatest emotional struggles, and your mother states to always know that she is like a guardian angel from the hereafter and that the clouds are beginning to break.

Note: Eileen had a very close bond with her Mom and at this time, was working and attending college at Cortland, New York, and was living away from the rest of the family. She was going to visit Disney World with her friends the week after our discernment.

Then George says:

There is a Frances with your Mom. I get the feeling also that Frances passes over young. Also, there's an Anne or Anna who says, 'You know me.'

Note: Frances is my cousin who died in her late 60s. Anne is Eileen's sister-in-law whose daughter Cathy saw Grandma McVeigh the night that she died.

George Anderson goes on to my son Jimmy:

There is talk about back concern and about your shoulder. I get the feeling it's your right shoulder. That's why she's picking on you. Also, watch yourself physically. Too much exercise is just as bad as too little. That's what your mother said. Plus, she also impresses on you to make sure you're getting enough rest.

Note: In January of that year, Jimmy had arthroscopic surgery on his right shoulder. He has also had back strain at times. However, he is in good physical condition and does work out regularly.

Then Anderson says to Jimmy:

I hear Daniel! Does that make sense? Passed on? Not family? Because he says, 'Not family.' He says, 'I know your Mom. This is Dan.' But, somebody came into the room and started singing 'Danny Boy' and said to me, 'Say what you're hearing.' And, of course, I didn't tell you what I was hearing, but I told you I heard the name Dan or Daniel. There is a feeling of friendship. Is that correct? But there's also a work connection. In any case, he says, he does thank you for being so good to him when he was on Earth. He says he's a youthful passer. He says, 'Yeah, I've met your mother in the hereafter.' You've always been a good friend and he's glad for the opportunity to come and say hello. He says you have felt he never got a chance in life, but he says, 'Remember, it's continuation, not termination.'

Note: Jim's friend Dan died of brain cancer when he was in his 30s.

Then George Anderson goes on:

Also, I keep seeing a nun in the room. Is someone in the family a nun?

Note: William McVeigh, Mom's father, had a cousin from Ireland who was a nun.

Then Anderson says to Theresa:

Your Mom says, 'Thanks for the planting.' Does that make sense? Did you keep it to yourself? Then Mom says, 'There's happy news around you.' Also, 'Keep up your faith and strength,' but, she says there's happy news around Theresa.

Note: Mom had an African violet plant on the shelf behind the kitchen sink. When Mom took sick, no one paid any attention to it. In fact, there was no plant there: just dirt in a flowerpot when Theresa and her family came to live at the house. Theresa told me that one day she got the strange feeling that someone was saying to her, 'Just water it.' Well, Theresa did just that and in no time the African violet reappeared and over the past few years it has continued to blossom and flower at regular intervals. Theresa didn't register any special happy news that George Anderson mentioned, but the encouragement for faith and strength she recognizes from Mom, for Theresa has two diabetic children and one mildly disabled child. Thank God they are all doing well.

Then:

I just saw white rosary beads appear before me and I saw Our Lady of Lourdes appear. Your Mom is aware-again to Theresa-that you brought her rosary with you, and it's in your bag. Because I don't want anybody to say, 'Well, he saw it.'

Note: When we all started down to visit George Anderson, Theresa said, 'I have Mom's rosary beads with me, and if Mom talks about them, I'll know she is there.' And Mom did expressly recognize Theresa as bringing them with her.

George Anderson continued with the following:

Your Mom keeps drifting me to the hereafter, and says 'Philomena is here.' Is that correct? But Mom says her baptismal name is Philomena, but she is known by another name. Mom says Millie is here: mother-in-law and your mother. Now, your Mom says Joe is here also. Your Dad Joseph is here. So both of your parents are on the other side with your wife. Wait, now Mom is saying, 'There's two!' She says, 'Joe and Joe.' There's a Joseph on earth she is calling to.

Yes, George looks to our son Joe.

You are being congratulated, because Mom drifted over to you and extended white roses to you. So you must be hearing some happy news that affects you personally, to do with your career. But your Mom insists it's two messages, one to do with career and one to do with family. There's a reason to celebrate with family because your mother states she wants you to know she is aware of your special celebration, because last year, you started thinking, 'Gee, I wish Mom was here to know about this.' Well apparently, she knows about it, whatever it is.

Note: When George Anderson started to speak about Joe and Joe, he paused for a second and said, "I'm confused!" Well, there are three Joes in our immediate family, my father, me, and our oldest son. Actually there are four! Joe's year-old son, our grandson, is also a Joe. In fact, when George Anderson spoke about a white rose celebration in the family, we all took it to mean little Joe. You see, Joe was born on April 17, 1996, just a month after Mom died. So the year later, 1997, at the discernment (April 16, 1997), Joe would be one year old. When little Joe was born, Mary Beth and our son Joe felt much anguish and sadness about Mom not being around at little Joe's birth. As we see, Mom was well aware of it and even visited Mary Beth shortly thereafter.

The other white rose celebration was directed to Joe as he was to receive his Ph.D. in December of 1997 from the University of Maryland.

I've stated previously, as George Anderson would be relating something from Mom, someone else would pop in to him to be recognized. Therefore, the next two descriptions came like staccato notes, one after another.

George Anderson says:

I keep hearing the name Frank, who passed on in the family. Wait, also the name Vincent, but was called by another name, because, this person is in the room claiming that you know his given name, Vincent. However, he is saying he really is known to everyone as Jimmy. If I'd have said James, everybody would say, 'No.' Jimmy goes on to say, 'I'm Uncle Jimmy—in the family, I'm known as Uncle Jimmy.'

Note: My Uncle Frank, my father's oldest brother, died at a relatively young age, in his 50s. I was about four or five years old, but I do remember him. All of the Ross clan called my Dad's second youngest brother Uncle Jimmy. He died while I was an intern at St. Francis Hospital in Poughkeepsie. I remember him very well, and he was always "Uncle Jimmy," never "Vincent."

Now, George looked to our youngest son, Nick:

I keep seeing books piling up around you, and there's talk of a graduation. Mom is saying she'll be there. She tells me you will be 'titled' and she congratulates you on that. I do feel a lot of stress around you, like you're almost at the finish line.

Your Mom speaks of a movement and a change of friends. Some are fading out of your life, and some people are growing into your life. I keep seeing covered wagons in front of you, the symbol of a new beginning.

Mom speaks of a wedding coming up—but definitely it's coming to pass. She says that certainly she will be there spiritually.

Note: Nick had moved to California before Mom died. He was attending the Institute of Transpersonal Psychology in Palo Alto. This was a big move for him and for the family. He was very busy studying and also writing his dissertation, looking forward to being awarded the title of "Doctor of Psychology." Also, Nick had met his fiancée, Christine, in California, and in fact, a wedding was being planned in August of that year of our discernment, 1997.

Then George reported once again from Mom, saying:

Margaret, Maggie, is here with her. And then she also keeps calling John. Passed on? Wait, she is saying John and Johnny, they are both with her. One pushes Uncle! Is there an Uncle John?

Now your Mom is also saying the name Dottie or Dorothy. Tell her you heard from me. Tell her you heard from Eileen.

Note: Maggie, Mom's Aunt Margaret, and her father's sister, died a few years ago. Also, I did write about Eileen's foster brother, Uncle John, and his three children who died in the house fire about a month after Mom died. They were great friends and John loved Eileen very much. Dottie, Dorothy Osborn, is our Theresa's mother-in-law, and she and Mom had a great deal of respect for each other.

Now George Anderson looked over to our daughter Nancy and said:

I keep seeing flowers all around you. Does that make sense? I don't know what it means because your mother puts all these beautiful flowers around you and she says, 'Do you understand?' But she goes on, 'When you come here you will see colors and flowers, species that you can't imagine.'

Note: Nancy is the Public Relations Director for The New York Botanical Garden in New York City. They have areas of the most beautiful and distinctive flowers from all over the world.

My only comment about George Anderson is that his gift of awareness of the deceased is a "Divine Manipulation," and a gift also to all of us from our Almighty Creator. My children and I came away knowing that our one and only wonderful Mom is alive and well in a special place of love and joy that we humans can't possibly imagine in our wildest and most exciting dreams.

After our session with George Anderson, my children and I went to a nearby restaurant to talk about and celebrate this extraordinary experience we had just been through. Emotions were high, actually jubilant. Each person was spilling over with the uncanniness of the details, but more than that, with the sense that Eileen had come to see us, to comfort us, and to be with us—just as we had hoped, and even known she would. I would be less than truthful if I claimed that we were not somewhere deep inside nervous about our encounter with George Anderson, afraid that "no one would show up," or that whomever did show up wouldn't be Eileen. However, she touched each one of us very profoundly and deeply with her precise and loving thoughts for us. I was overwhelmed with the belief that she was there, speaking to us and letting us know that she would be waiting for us and watching over us.

From her reference to our daughter Eileen's going on vacation, to Jimmy's operation on his shoulder, to our trip to

Hawaii, to acknowledging the beauty of her new life in comparison to Nancy's New York Botanical Garden, to Happy Birthday to Joe, to acknowledgment of Nick's coming marriage, and finally telling Theresa to pray the rosary that she brought...from all of these things came the amazing reality of her closeness and ever-present love and existence in our lives.

Not only was Eileen present there, but so were unexpected people like my Uncle Jimmy (Vincent) and my son's friend Dan. And would I have traveled down to Long Island with my heart in my throat just to find out that our affectionate dog Bill was drooling all over the afterlife? As it turned out, it was a most heartwarming event of the evening, knowing how Mom had loved this dog, and how with his love he welcomed her to her new home.

From the minute George Anderson said, "A female presence has come into the room..." the air was electric. Did I need George to tell us that Eileen was "still there?" No. I knew it just as strongly before we went as after. But did "hearing from her" once again make a difference in our hearts? Every ladybug, every mayfly, every sign that brings her close to me in the course of a day makes a difference in my loneliness. That's, I believe, why she sends them. And that's why I accept them and hold them close. Our eternal existence is carried on in the love which flourished from that first day in Poughkeepsie to each moment that I speak to her in my heart.

My wonderful Eileen,

Not only will I remember our beautiful and joyous vacation in Hawaii, but I will always carry in my heart the immense joy and love of our life together here on Earth.

I love you.

Joe

EPILOGUE

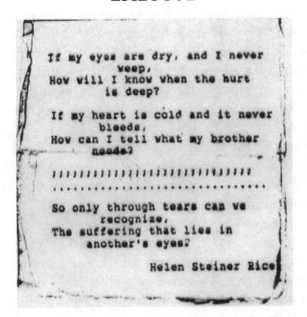

If my eyes are dry, and I never
    weep,
How will I know when the hurt
    is deep?

If my heart is cold and it never
    bleeds,
How can I tell what my brother
    needs?

So only through tears can we
    recognize,
The suffering that lies in
    another's eyes?

                        Helen Steiner Rice

I found this poem in my Eileen's pocketbook. In a very limited way, it mirrors her loving and compassionate character. She is one of the world's special people. An expression of God's unconditional love for all of us— expressed to the world through His many, many unknown, imperfect and caring messengers of this world. My Eileen is one of them.

I've been trying to explain, describe my Eileen's and my love for each other—because through our love I have begun to realize, to understand more fully that the only magic in this universe is created out of LOVE.

When Eileen and I were young and frivolous and outrageously happy, I was the more boisterous and uninhibited one. Every day I would hug her and tell her I loved her; finally only able to express it in, "I love you so much, I can't even tell you how much. It's more than I can say." Some such "stuff" as that. But throughout these present years of my overwhelming human loneliness for her, I have learned just how much I do love her. I love her with all of God's love that He gave to us; an infinite, spiritual, divine, eternal love. I would do anything for her to make her happy. As a phrase in a show song says, *"I want to be happy, but I won't be happy 'till I make you happy too."*

Which finally brings me to what I believe in my heart. There are only two things that actually count in this world. They are one, faith and two, love. That is all that we can take with us on our next journey.

One—if you have faith, then you know beyond any doubt, that you were created by a perfect, loving omnipotence (God), Who isn't just toying with you for the few years you have on this earth, but Who loves you forever as you are and with all of your blemishes; Who is hoping to instill in you, His love that you should express (give) fully and openly to everyone. And I mean <u>EVERYONE</u>!!! If you are lucky enough to enjoy such a marvelous, inner-faith, a faith which transfers even to earthly matters, than it is easy enough to let—

Two—Let LOVE evolve in your soul. Don't imprison your soul during your natural earthly existence. Even if you haven't, unfortunately, experienced love in your troubled life, you can open your heart and let your soul absorb the immense beauty and love that there is in this sometimes difficult world.

Because of this omnipotent love we are assured that He allows us to receive His blessings in a concrete and undeniable way from His paradise through our dead—but living loved ones who have crossed over from this earthly human existence. One would have to be a completely stubborn and narrow-minded individual to deny the thousands and thousands of communications from God's paradise.

Throughout this book, I describe the amazing and beautiful ways God has allowed my Eileen to contact me, enlightening my sad and lonely final years.

As I have stated, I cry every day for the human want of her here with me. (I don't try to cry, but tears fill my eyes at the most unlikely times.) However He hasn't left me bare, for He has "shown me" as I asked Him, that my sweetest Eileen, His gift to me is not dead, but happy and alive, waiting to be reunited with me in an eternal paradise. I haven't earned it. It is His gift of creation and love for all of us.

There is no death!

J.D. Ross Jr. M.D.

BIBLIOGRAPHY

Altea, Rosemary, *The Eagle and the Rose*, Warmer Vision
    Books, A Time Warner Co.
Anderson, Ken, *Coincidences, Chance or Fate,* Blanford,
    1995
Atwater, P.M.H., Ph.D., *Beyond the Light*, Avon Books, 1994
Bascom, Lionel, G. and Barbara Loecher, *By the Light*, Avon
    Books, New York, 1995
Brinkley, Dannion and Paul Perry, *Saved by the Light*, Harper
    Paperbacks, 1994
Brinkley, Dannion and Paul Perry, *At Peace in the Light*,
    Harper Paperback, 1995
Brown, Raphael, *Saints Who Saw Mary*, Tan Books and
    Publishers, Inc., 1955
Browne, Mary T., *Life After Death*, Ivy Books, New York,
    1994
Coffin, William Sloane, *The Heart Is a Little to the Left*,
    University Press of New England, 1999
Cohen, Sherry Suib, *Looking for the Other Side*, Clarkson
    Potter Publishers, New York, 1997
Cruz, Joan Carroll, *The Incorruptibles*, Tan Books and
    Publishers, Inc., 1977
DeGrandis, Robert, S.S.J., *The Gift of Miracles*, Servant
    Publications, 1991
Doughtery, Fred, *Fast Lane to Heaven*, Hampton Roads
    Publishing Company, Inc., 2001
Eadie, Betty J., *Embraced by the Light*, Bantam Books, 1992
Edward, John, *Crossing Over*, Jodere Group, Inc., 2001
Edward, John, *One Last Time*, Berkley Books, New York,
    1998
Fenchuk, Gary W., *Timeless Wisdom*, Cake Eaters, Inc., 1995
Fenwick, Peter, M.D., and Elizabeth Fenwick, M.D., *The
    Truth in the Light*, Berkley Books, New York, 1995

Fildman, Christian, *God's Gentle Rebels*, Crossroad, New York, 1995

Ford, Arielle, *Hot Chocolate for the Mystical Soul*, A Plume Book, 1998

Fulghum, Robert, *Words I Wish I Wrote*, Cliff Street Books, Harper Collins Publishers, 1997

Gittelson, Bernard, *Intangible Evidence*, Simon and Schuster, Inc., 1987

Greaves, Helen, *Testimony of Light*, Neville Spearman Publishers, The C.W. Daniel Co., Limited, Essex, England, 1970-1995

Guggenheim, Bill and Judy, *Hello From Heaven*, Bantam Books, 1996

Halberstam, Yetta, and Judith Leventhal, *Small Miracles*, Adams Media Corp., 1997

Halbertson, et. al., *Small Miracles II*, Adams Media Corp., 1998

Haraldsson, Erlendur, Ph.D., *Modern Miracles*, Hastings House Book Publishers, 1987

Harris, Barbara, and Lionel Bascom, *Full Circle*, Pocket Books, 1990

Hopcke, Robert H., *There Are No Accidents*, Riverhead Books, New York, 1997

Jovanovic, Pierre, *An Inquiry into the Existence of Guardian Angels*, M. Evans and Co., Inc., New York, 1993

Jung, C.J., Translation by R.F.C. Hull, *Synchronicity – An Acausal Connecting Principle*, Bollinger Series, Princeton University Press, 1973

Kubler-Ross, Elisabeth, *Death is of Vital Importance*, Station Hill Press, 1995

Kubler-Ross, Elisabeth, *On Death and Dying*, MacMillan Publishing Co., Inc., 1969

Kubler-Ross, Elisabeth, *The Tunnel and the Light*, Marlowe and Company, 1999

Kubler-Ross, Elisabeth, *The Wheel of Life*, Scribner, 1997

LaGrand, Louis E., Ph.D., *After Death Communications (Final Farewells)*, Llewllyn Publications, 1997

Lawson, Lee, *Visitations from the Afterlife*, Harper Collins Publishers, Inc., 2000

Martin, Joel, and Patricia Romanowski, *Love Beyond Life*, Harper Collins Publishers, 1997

Martin, Joel, and Patricia Romanowski, *We Don't Die*, Berkley Books, 1989

McKenna, Briege, O.S.C., and Henry Libersat, *Miracles Do Happen*, St. Martin's Paperbacks, 1987

Millman, Dan, and Doug Childers, *Divine Interventions*, Daybreak Books, 1999

Moody, Raymond A.J., M.D., and Paul Perry, *The Last Laugh*, Hampton Roads Publishing Company, 1999

Moody, Raymond A.J., M.D., and Paul Perry, *Life After Life*, Bantam Books, 1975

Moody, Raymond A.J., M.D., and Paul Perry, *The Light Beyond*, Bantam Books, 1988

Moody, Raymond A.J., M.D., and Paul Perry, *Reflections on Life After Life*, Bantam Books, 1977

Moody, Raymond A.J., M.D., *Reunions*, Ivy Books, 1993

Morrissey, Dianne, Ph.D., *Anyone Can See the Light*, Stillpoint Publishing, 1996

Morse, Melvin, M.D., and Paul Perry, *Closer to the Light*, Ivy Books, 1990

Morse, Melvin, M.D., and Paul Perry, *Parting Visions*, Harper Paperbacks, 1994

Osis, Karlis, Ph.D., and Erlendur Haraldsson, Ph.D., *At the Hour of Death*, Hastings House Book Publishers, 1977

Peale, Norman V., *Life Beyond Death*, Zondervan Publishing House, 1996

Peck, M.Scott, M.D., *The Road Less Traveled*, Simon and Schuster, A Touchstone Book, 1978

Peterson, Robert, *Out of Body Experiences*, Hampton Roads Publishing Company, Inc., 1997

Price, Jan, *The Other Side of Death*, Fawcett Columbine, New York, 1996

Ray, Veronica, *Miracles on Main Street*, St. Martin's Paperbacks, 1996

Ring, Kenneth, Ph.D., *Heading Toward Omega – In Search of the Meaning of the Near-Death Experience*, Quill William Morrow, 1984

Ring, Kenneth, Ph.D., *Life at Death – A Scientific Investigation of the Near-Death Experience*, Coward, McCann and Geoghegan, 1980

Ring, Kenneth, Ph.D., and Evelyn E. Valarino, *Lessons from the Light*, Insight Books, Plenum Press, New York and London, 1998

Ritchie, Jean, *Death's Door*, Dell Publishing, 1994

Ritchie, G. George, Jr., M.D., *My Life After Dying – Becoming Alive to Universal Love*, Hampton Roads Publishing Company, Inc., 1991

Rogers, Sandra, *Lessons from the Light*, Warner Books, 1995

Ruffin, C. Bernard, *Padre Pio: The True Story*, Our Sunday Visitor Publishing Division, Our Sunday Visitor, Inc., 1991

Shallis, Michael, *The Electric Connection*, New Amsterdam Books, New York 1988

Sherman, Harold, *The Dead Are Alive*, Fawcett Gold Medal, New York, 1981

Smith, Mark, *Auras*, Llewellyn Publications, 1997

Stearn, Jess, *Edgar Cayce, The Sleeping Prophet*, Bantam Books, 1967

Steiger, Brad, and Sherry Hanson Steiger, *Dog Miracles*, Adams Media Corp., 2001

Sugrue, Thomas, *There is a River – The Story of Edgar Cayce*, Dell Publishing Co., 1945

Sutherland, Cherie, *Reborn in the Light*, Bantam Books, 1995

Swann, Ingo, *The Great Apparitions of Mary*, Crossroad Publishing Co., 1996

Tart, Charles T. (editor), *Body, Mind, Spirit*, Hampton Roads Press, 1997

Mother Theresa, *No Greater Love*, New World Library, Novato, California, 1997

Treece, Patricia, *Messengers – After-Death Appearances of Saints and Mystics*, Our Sunday Visitor Publishing Division, Our Sunday Visitor, Inc., 1995

Treece, Patricia, *Nothing Short of a Miracle*, Our Sunday Visitor Publishing Division, Our Sunday Visitor, Inc., 1998

Trobridge, George, Revised by Richard H. Tafel, Sr. and Jr., *Swedenborg: Life and Teaching*, The Swedenborg Foundation, New York, 1992

Van Praag, James, *Healing Grief*, A Dutton Book, 1998

Van Praag, James, *Reaching to Heaven*, A Signet Book, 1999

Van Praag, James, *Talking to Heaven*, A Dutton Book, 1997

Vaughan, Alan, *Incredible Coincidence*, Ballantine Books, New York, 1979

Wakefield, Dan, *Expect A Miracle*, Harper, San Francisco, Harper Collins Publishers, 1995

Weil, Andrew, M.D., *Spontaneous Healing*, Alfred A. Knopf, New York, 1995

Williams, William E., *Unbounded Light*, Nicolas-Hays, Inc. 1992

Wills-Brandon, Carla, Ph.D., *One Last Hug Before I Go (The Mystery and Meaning of Deathbed Visions)*, Health Communications, Inc., 2000

Wilson, Ian, *The After Death Experience*, Quill William Morrow, 1987